Schooling
in the Workplace

Schooling in the Workplace

How Six of the World's
Best Vocational Education Systems
Prepare Young People for Jobs and Life

NANCY HOFFMAN

HARVARD EDUCATION PRESS
CAMBRIDGE, MASSACHUSETTS

Library of Congress Control Number 2011937679

Paperback ISBN 978-1-61250-111-6

Library Edition ISBN 978-1-61250-112-3

Published by Harvard Education Press,
an imprint of the Harvard Education Publishing Group

Harvard Education Press
8 Story Street
Cambridge, MA 02138

Cover Design: Sarah Henderson

The typefaces used in this book are Bembo and Helvetica Neue.

Contents

CONTENTS

Foreword

In response to the deep and pervasive economic distress facing the United States recently, numerous proposals have been put forward for renewed economic development. Some have focused on tax incentives, others on infrastructure, others on easier access to capital and business opportunities, and still others on entrepreneurship. Each of these has merit, but it is clear that the most effective long-term economic development strategy must begin with a serious and systemic examination of our public education system, leading to the swift and substantive changes needed to dramatically improve student achievement and better prepare larger and larger numbers of students for good-paying jobs and stable careers.

To this end, in *Schooling in the Workplace,* Nancy Hoffman provides us not only with a cogent and effective analysis of the problem but also with practical, affordable, and intelligent solutions. If acted on, the proposals she details here could lay a path toward increased opportunity for individuals and the country as a whole.

As Hoffman indicates, there is no more urgent and important economic development strategy than making sure that our K–12 education system, our higher education systems, and the private sector, up to now largely working in silos, work together to redesign education and career opportunities for young people, so they will have the education and skills necessary for economic self-sufficiency. In earlier decades, a vastly different economic system relied on traditional vocational education and strictly academic programs that prepared young people for careers—sufficient to address the need to link education and skills with jobs and economic stability. This is simply no longer the case. We now need more meaningful partnerships between education and business and an end to the artificial distinction between "academic" and "vocational" preparation.

The commonsense and practical solutions Hoffman lays out are grounded in her serious examination and understanding of the changes in the global labor force and are reinforced by a review of global labor force data, economic projections, and data on educational outcomes. She couples this with a study of the educational and economic systems in countries around the world and concrete examples of cross-sector partnerships and experiences drawn from six nations: Australia, Austria, Germany, the Netherlands, Norway, and Switzerland. Anticipating American readers' skepticism about the relevance of such international experiences, Hoffman describes a variety of organizations that effectively support employers in educating young people and enable them to take on the challenges of a satisfying and productive career. She outlines the stark connection to performance. Currently, twelve Organization for Economic Cooperation and Development (OECD) countries have higher numbers of upper secondary school "completers" than does the United States. She contrasts this with U.S. performance, which has slipped dramatically in standard measures of postsecondary completion. Once a leader, the United States has now fallen to twelfth among OECD countries in the share of adults ages twenty-five to thirty-four with postsecondary degrees. This is a prescription for failure.

One specific case presented here, which exemplifies the potential educational role for business institutions that is central to Hoffman's book, is that of Swisscom, the largest phone and Internet provider in Switzerland. Swisscom educates more than 800 16-to-19-year-old apprentices among its nearly 20,000 employees. Chosen from 7,000 applicants, these young people bring new energy, ideas, and productivity to the company, and many become permanent employees and high performers. For adolescents, being a Swisscom apprentice means a salary, a chance to gain competence and experience in the world of work, and the opportunity to make an effective transition from the school experience to the world of work and responsibility. In Switzerland, almost everyone completes upper secondary school, the equivalent of a year or two of college in the United States.

My own company, IBM, is celebrating its centennial in 2011. While incorporated and headquartered in the United States, it does business in 170 countries, including Switzerland and all of the other countries featured in Hoffman's book. IBM has many career opportunities in these nations for young people with a strong two-year degree in the highly competitive and well-paid IT field, but so do many other companies. This is most certainly not restricted to those in any one field of endeavor. Young people with skills and educational preparation specifically aligned with the actual skills needed in the workplace can look forward to stable careers or success in pursuing either a BA or BS degree. They need not choose; they can do both.

This is why IBM has begun to work with education, business, and political leadership on a new model of education. A core component is the concept of a grade 9–14 school with a curriculum matched to the Common Core Standards and the actual skills needed in the workplace. A student graduating from such a school would not only have a high school diploma but would enjoy important additional benefits: a high-quality AAS degree, the promise of a stable career, and the skills to succeed in a career or in higher education. This type of solution is being created by IBM in cooperation with the New York City Department of Education and the City University of New York, but this need not be an opportunity available to just a few students in a certain area. It can be a solution for many.

With more than fourteen million jobs to be created over the next ten years for young people with AA or AAS degrees, we as a nation must find a way to reform our K–12 and higher education systems in tandem with the private sector to achieve significantly better results. If we do, we will be more competitive as a nation, and many more young people will benefit. The practical solutions proposed in this book will help us achieve that end.

Stanley S. Litow
Vice President of Corporate Citizenship and Corporate Affairs and president, IBM International Foundation

Acknowledgements

My greatest debt for what I have learned about transitioning young people to healthy and productive adulthood and "working life" is to the Education and Training Policy (ETP) unit at the OECD. As a member of the country expert teams for several of the *Learning for Jobs* (LFJ) studies of vocational education (VET), I was introduced to VET systems first hand by cordial officials, teachers and students in several countries, and I benefited greatly from the lively debriefing discussions led by the OECD's LFJ project manager, the economist, Simon Field and his gifted colleagues, Viktoria Kis, Malgorzata Kuczera and Kathrin Hoeckel. I am also grateful to Deborah Roseveare, head of ETP, and Beatriz Pont, senior analyst, who encouraged me to spend several months at the OECD in 2010 and made a wide variety of international resources available to me. I have adapted a number of passages in this book from the OECD *Learning for Jobs* final report and country studies in the hope that a U.S. writer can "translate" the rich materials from these studies so that they link with and influence thinking about policy and practice in the United States.

A number of people, first among them Stefan Wolter, professor of economics at the University of Bern, went out of their way to respond to my many questions and requests. Stefan not only answered e-mailed questions immediately and with precision, but also set up my several-days visit to apprenticeship companies and Swiss research and teaching institutes in Bern in September, 2010. Stefan's enthusiasm for VET is contagious, and his modesty about his own influential research on VET, and the role he plays in Swiss and international education circles is admirable. In addition, Melanie Ehren, faculty member in the Department of Educational Organization and Management, University of Twente, Netherlands, a long visit to Rotterdam in April 2010, assembled researchers, arranged visits to several impressive VET worksites and schools, and patiently answered questions.

Last but certainly not least, I am deeply grateful to my U.S. colleagues at Jobs for the Future, the Harvard Graduate School of Education (HGSE), the Harvard Education Press, and the Nellie Mae Education Foundation. JFF's President Marlene Seltzer granted me two several month leaves to participate in the OECD studies. And JFF's portfolio, comprised of initiatives on workforce development and education policy and practice, gave me a frame for my analysis of U.S. VET policy. Douglas Clayton, executive director of the Harvard Education Press, took on support for this book as his personal mission. From HGSE, Bob Schwartz, my husband, shared some of my travels with the OECD, and engaged in endless conversations about the enviable VET systems we learned about. So this is much more than a cosmetic "thank you to the spouse." Bob actually enjoyed his wife's project, it is fair to say, and contributed a short piece to this book resulting from *his* service on the LFJ German study team. Ideas from our work for OECD influenced Harvard's *Pathways to Prosperity* report, of which Bob was coauthor. Finally, Nicholas Donohue, president of New England's Nellie Mae Education Foundation, funded an initial meeting in the United States in preparation for my writing about VET. He has been a friend to this project from the start.

Introduction

What is VET? Vocational education and training (VET) helps prepare people for work, develops their skills while at work and changes what they are doing so that they can work in new or different occupations.

—*Yvonne Hillier, University of Brighton (NCVER), 2009*

I am reaching the end of a career spent largely working with others to help increase the number of low-income and first-generation young people prepared for, attending, and finishing college. In the mid-1960s, as a civil rights worker in Mississippi with other college-educated young people, I taught about social justice in the movement's "freedom schools," sharing the "religion" of education with children eager to have jobs right out of high school and to become the next generation of leaders in their communities. Many of them succeeded with just a high school diploma, but things are not the way they used to be. As many before me have noted, the high school education that might have garnered a good job in the 1960s and '70s can no longer be depended upon. To have the knowledge and financial means to participate in civil society and to support a family, just about all young people need some postsecondary education. But despite wide knowledge about this, currently only about four in ten adults in the United States have an AA or BA degree by their mid-twenties, and the rates of degree completion in this country have only budged a tad upward in four decades, while the rest of the world has caught up and a number of countries have surpassed us.

I despair when I think about the prospects of the *forgotten half*, those young Americans who—for reasons of poverty, poor-quality high school education, no faith in the future, lack of engagement in traditional schooling—are adrift in a harsh economy with no structures or supports as they grow from being adolescents at school into adulthood. Compared with other relatively strong economies, the United States pays unskilled workers low wages, has little job protection, and provides few social and income supports for young people struggling with schooling and employment.[1] This country can and should do more—and better.

Across the developed countries today, educators, policy makers, and economists recognize that the new "knowledge economy" demands new and higher levels of skills than the twentieth-century high school or upper secondary school provided. Young people with aspirations to white-collar, "middle-skill" jobs in high-growth areas such as health care, high tech, engineering, and finance, as well as those choosing the old trades, need more sophisticated skills and knowledge than ever before, ranging from the ability to problem solve in messy situations to statistics to technical reading and writing. Some countries are doing well by young people, continuing to prepare almost all of them for good jobs requiring twenty-first-century skills, protecting them from the current economic crisis, and transitioning them into the labor force smoothly and relatively quickly. This is not the case in the United States.

Many adults are suffering in the economic crisis, but it is having a disproportionate impact on young people in the United States, and we are doing little to protect and support them. In 2008, the United States had a youth unemployment rate of about 11 percent, while the average calculated by the Organization for Economic Cooperation and Development (OECD), the international organization that provides comparative data on trends around the world, was 14.4 percent. By July 2010, the U.S. rate had risen above the OECD average to about 19.1 percent, and it is continuing to rise. It doesn't have to be this way. During that same year, Australia, Austria, Canada, Denmark, Germany, Japan, Korea, the Netherlands, Norway, and Switzerland were doing substantially better, lower than 10 percent. (The Netherlands was lowest in the second quarter of 2010. See figure I.1.) Those countries had lower rates to begin with and smaller-than-average increases.

In addition, international comparative data from *Jobs for Youth*, a sixteen-country OECD study on transitioning youth from schooling to stable first employment (within five years of leaving education), puts the United States at about the average among the OECD countries. Given

2

FIGURE I.1   Significant deterioration of the youth unemployment rate in
2008–2010

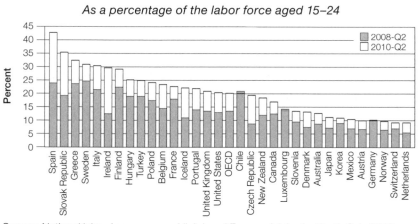

As a percentage of the labor force aged 15–24

Source: National labor force surveys, High Level Forum of Jobs for Youth Oslo 2010

the shaky economies of members of the comparison group, such as
Greece, Italy, Portugal, and Spain, and the fact that the data was col-
lected in the early 2000s, so before the economic crisis, the United
States should and could be higher up in the rankings. We do better
than some European countries with what the study calls "high performers," but about one-third of U.S. youth fall into the categories
"youth left behind" and "poorly integrated new entrants." *Left-behind*
youth spend most of the five years in unemployment or inactivity; and
new entrants move in and out of employment, unemployment, and inactivity, signaling difficulties in settling on a promising career path.[2]

For youth with low skills and without a high school diploma, entry into the job market is nearly impossible today. And dropping out
has reached epidemic proportions in some areas of the United States.
Twelve OECD countries now have higher numbers of upper secondary school completers than we do (see figure I.2). (The comparison is
with a more advanced level of learning than in U.S. high schools. Upper secondary schools generally start at age sixteen and end around

3

nineteen; students exit with academic and vocational achievement levels, respectively, comparable to a year of four-year college or a two-year community college occupational diploma. .) A second and even more troubling reason young people in the United States may be experiencing trouble finding jobs in an increasingly competitive market is that they are not achieving academically at acceptable levels. On the OECD's Program for International Student Assessment (PISA), which tests a sample of fifteen-year-olds across a wide range of countries every three years in math, science, and literacy, the U.S. performance over four rounds of tests has been consistently mediocre. In the most recent round of testing (2009), the United States scored only a small increment above average. One important distinction of PISA is that it asks young people to apply their knowledge, and so it is a better indicator of readiness for the demands of the workplace and challenging postsecondary schooling than the more traditional discipline-based tests of content.

Countries that are doing much better by their young people—supporting them to achieve academically at higher levels, keeping them in school, and, most importantly, structuring the transition from school to work so that almost everyone has training for an initial career and enters the workforce smoothly—share two characteristics:

- They have special youth policies; they see the younger generations as important to support, protect, and engage with as an investment in future prosperity.

- And in partnership with employers and unions, they educate from 40 percent to 75 percent of their young people in a vocational education system that links education and labor market needs and includes substantial learning in the workplace.

Youth policies—sometimes guarantees of schooling coupled with work experience, sometimes with sanctions for nonparticipation—send strong signals about the necessity to prepare for productive adulthood. Countries with strong vocational education and training (VET) pathways also have high rates of upper secondary completion. Austria, Germany, and Switzerland, for example, have the majority of students in their VET systems and have graduation rates above 90 percent.[3]

FIGURE I.2 School completion: U.S. rate has stagnated while most industrialized countries have improved

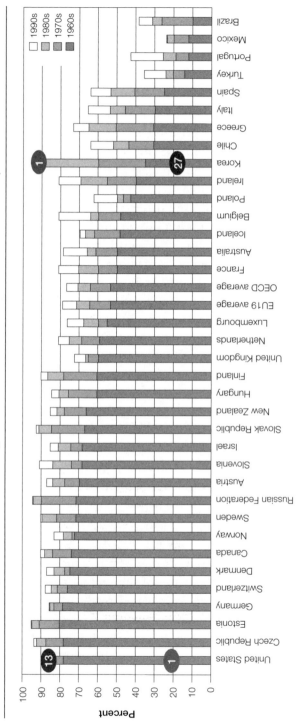

Note: Approximated by percentage of persons with high school or equivalent qualifications in the age groups of 55–64, 45–55, 35–44, and 25–34 years.

Source: Andreas Schleicher, "Science Competencies for Tomorrow's World: Seeing School Systems Through the Prism of PISA, Washington, 4 December 2007" (Paris: OECD, 2010), PowerPoint presentation, slide 7, www.oecd.org/edu/pisa. Used with permission.

In short, the smartest and quickest route to a wide variety of occupations *for the majority of young people in the successful countries*—not a default for failing students—is a vocational program that integrates work and learning. The countries doing the best by their young people have a different mind-set than we do about education. The purpose is not "college for all," as in the United States today, but rather to provide the education and training young people need to prepare for a career, or calling. This distinction may seem subtle, but it is not. An education system that in partnership with employers holds itself accountable not only for career preparation but for moving young people into productive roles in the labor force has a different orientation than one in which completion of a degree or credential is the end point of the education system's responsibility. This book is written out of a desire to provoke discussion in the United States about the features of strong vocational education systems. When the United States was a north star for other countries in education, we could afford to ignore education policies and practices elsewhere. Now it is time for us to look hard at ourselves and at more successful countries.

CAREER AND TECHNICAL EDUCATION IN THE UNITED STATES

One piece of data that may surprise U.S. readers is that when the OECD charts the proportion of students across countries engaged in vocational education and training as opposed to academic general education, the United States is not on the chart. (See figure I.3.) The United States would show up as having no VET or career and technical education (CTE) at all. This is because while about one in five high school students concentrates in an occupational area, the course requirements are a small proportion of the high school diploma. Precedence goes to being "college and career ready." High school CTE has as its purpose to allow students to explore a career and to motivate and engage at-risk students to stay in school, while providing the basic math, reading, and writing skills required for postsecondary education. While CTE programs in low performing districts tend to have higher high school completion rates than the non–CTE curriculum, that is a very low bar. For a host of reasons explored in this book—not the least

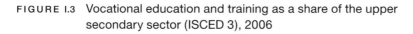

FIGURE I.3 Vocational education and training as a share of the upper secondary sector (ISCED 3), 2006

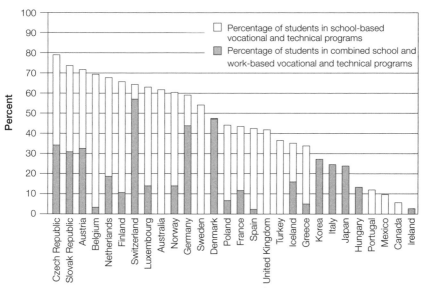

☐ Percentage of students in school-based vocational and technical programs

▨ Percentage of students in combined school and work-based vocational and technical programs

Source: Recreated from OECD, *Learning for Jobs: OECD Reviews of Vocational Education and Training* (Paris: OECD Publishing, 2010), figure 2, http://dx.doi.org/10.1787/9789264087460-en. Used with permission.

of which is that too many young people go off to college unprepared and bored with the prospect of more school—CTE could be doing much more, and not just for struggling students.

Neither a terminal high school vocational diploma nor credits from a community college will solve the problem of the "forgotten half" if the way learning takes place does not change. Students do have a strong interest in career preparation; that is not the issue. A significant proportion of American high school and college students intend to pursue employment that does not require a BA. Many begin by enrolling in career and technical programs at the secondary level, and then attempt to gain in-depth technical training at a community college. At all postsecondary levels (certificate, associate's, and bachelor's), more undergraduate degree seekers concentrate in career fields than academic subjects. Over 40 percent of college freshmen start in community colleges, as do the majority of low-income students and students of color. Most of these enroll in occupational programs.

Unfortunately, many of these students—especially those young people who have dutifully graduated from high school but have low to middling grades—are not prepared to complete a community college degree with value in the labor market. Most will be placed in non-credit developmental education courses from which dropout rates are very high. The competitive career pathways such as nursing, engineering technology, IT, and the like have entrance hurdles *after* community college matriculation. In other words, to enter these occupations, students must have already demonstrated proficiency in nonremedial general education courses such as mathematics and biology. Some programs select on the basis of prior work experience as well. And many have waiting lists and so can be very selective, as is the case with nursing and other areas in the health professions.

In addition, very few programs have workplace learning opportunities that resemble in any way those in the strong VET countries. Not only does workplace learning as part of school give participants a leg up in applying for jobs, there is strong evidence that such experiences help young people get a stronger start on adulthood and make it more transparent why certain skills, competencies, and knowledge are worth mastering. With some experience of the work world in high school and community college and more sense of what their future holds, the "other half" might take better advantage of what community colleges offer by way of certificate and applied associate's degree programs.

But despite the evidence of the value of workplace learning, such opportunities are not available to all who want them, nor is quality evaluated against widely accepted standards. For the average student in either a high school or community college CTE program, internships are scattershot, and workplace experiences of any depth and extent are the exception, not the rule. U.S. schools do not have systematized connections with employers, nor do employers see it in their self-interest to provide workplace learning. Compared with that of other countries, formal CTE at either the high school or community college level has little employer or union buy-in and almost no tradition of apprenticeship except in unionized trades (e.g., plumbing, construction, electrical, automotive). Only in rare cases are employers involved in designing a curriculum, assessing student competencies, or providing opportunities for sustained work experience. The hard truth is that neither educators nor employers in the United States take much responsibility for guiding young people into careers, and in most high schools and many community colleges, career education remains remote from the workaday world of the office, shop, or hospital floor. (Some promising exceptions to this dismal picture are reviewed in the conclusion to this book.)

LEARNING FOR JOBS

In 2007, the OECD, at the request of the ministers of the thirty OECD countries, launched a study of vocational education and training called *Learning for Jobs*. The simple project title points to a major complexity: that economic prosperity and social cohesion depend on an appropriately skilled and employed workforce. The OECD policy review of VET includes seventeen countries: Australia, Austria, Belgium (Flanders), the Czech Republic, Germany, Hungary, Ireland, Korea, Mexico, Norway, Sweden, Switzerland, the United Kingdom (England and Wales), and the United States (South Carolina and Texas), with shorter reports on Chile and the People's Republic of China.

In 2008, I was an expert participant in the OECD *Learning for Jobs* studies of VET in Norway and Sweden, and in 2005 served on an OECD team making recommendations about improving equity of outcomes in Hungary, where many disadvantaged young people are tracked into a VET system that often is a dead end. I also spent three months in early 2010 in the Education and Training Policy Division of the OECD, where I had the luxury of studying these reports and other OECD policy research and talking to researchers, visiting ministry officials, and educators about vocational education and training across a good number of the thirty OECD countries.

While I was at the OECD, the *Learning for Jobs* team was completing the final country reviews of Germany, as well as of Texas and South Carolina. Simultaneously, the Directorate for Employment, Labor, and Social Affairs (DELSA) was releasing the final volumes of *Jobs for Youth*, a sixteen-country study of transitions from school to employment, along with a complementary report requested by the OECD ministers in response to the jobs crisis entitled *Helping Youth to Get a Firm Foothold in the Labor Market*. For additional context, see box "Population points."

A major concern in the studies, each of which is a separate small book, is that despite the declining size of the youth cohort and retirements of the aging population, which should be opening the job market to young people, far too many still remain at risk of not finding appropriate employment. The country studies make recommendations for creating, maintaining, or reinforcing "polices aimed at better equipping young people with the skills required by the labor market and helping them accomplish a successful transition from school to work."[4] The supplementary report adds urgency to these recommendations. It posits that "the current severe economic downturn is posing daunting challenges to young individuals in the OECD labour markets. The transition from school to work is going to be particularly difficult for the new generation of entrants in the labour market . . . Low-skilled youth who, even before the crisis erupted, already experienced multiple barriers in fully integrating the labour market, are now at high risk of inactivity and potentially of exclusion."[5]

WHAT IS VET?

For readers unfamiliar with what I call in this book "strong VET systems," here are the basic outlines. The key factors that make a system strong are:

- The system is formed through public/private partnerships between the state, schools, employers, and labor unions.
- Employers have a major role, usually codified in a legal framework, in defining the qualifications required for clusters of occupations in their sectors of the economy.
- With support from organizations representing their occupational sector, employers take responsibility for building curriculum and developing and carrying out assessments.
- With employer participation, a government education agency usually at the national level is responsible for standardization of the system and for quality control and improvement.

Population Points

One note about reading this book with the United States as a reference point—in relation to the United States, two facts are useful: the populations of the comparison countries and their immigrant populations.

First, their populations make them units about the size of states. For example, Texas and Australia each have over 20 million people, and the Netherlands has the same population as Florida (17 million). At 8.3 million, Austria is about the size of New Jersey; Norway (4.8 million) is just a bit smaller than Colorado; and Switzerland (7.8 million) is almost the size of Virginia.

Second, they are homes to immigrants: Norway, the Netherlands, and Australia have immigrant populations of about 10 percent, 20 percent, and 25 percent, respectively, and 25 percent of the Oslo population is foreign born. Switzerland's foreign-born population is 22 percent.

However, it is also important for readers to know that immigration status does not necessarily result in low achievement. In Denmark, children of migrant families with similar family situations to Danes have a significantly lower dropout rate.[a] When Dutch researchers control for individual, family, and school characteristics, ethnic minorities are not more likely to drop out. In fact, students from ethnic minorities are 18 percent less at risk of leaving school after graduating from lower secondary.[b]

[a] B. Colding, "Educational Progression of Second-Generation Immigrants and Immigrant Children," *Economics of Education Review* 28: 434–443, in Cecilia S. Lyche, "Taking On the Completion Challenge: A Literature Review on Policies to Prevent Drop Out and Early School Leaving" (unpublished paper, OECD, Paris, 2010), 17.
[b] T. Traag and R. van der Velden, *Early School-Leaving in the Netherlands: The Role of Student-, Family- and School Factors for Early School-Leaving in Lower Secondary Education* (Maastricht: Research Center for Education and the Labor Market, 2008), in Lyche, "Taking On the Completion Challenge," 16.

With this system in place, employers open their enterprises to young people usually starting at around age sixteen.

Most familiar to U.S. readers would be what are called *dual* or *apprenticeship* systems, the classic structure where students spend three days a week at work and two days in school. (*Dual* refers to learning at school and at a workplace.) But trainees, interns, or apprentices can also spend blocks of time learning in the workplace or progress from all school to some mix of work and school to all work in the course of attaining a qualification. These "alternance" arrangements last anywhere from one to four years as the young person attains skills, knowledge, and competencies, and most result in making the student eligible to choose a pathway into technical higher education or even a university.

VET students do not give up studying general subjects by choosing to focus on a career. A key role of the state is ensuring that the training remains broad and does not become too job- and company-specific, a goal that employers in most systems also embrace. A shorthand for this goal is that students are taking up a "calling," or a vocation in the sense of an occupation toward which they are particularly drawn or inclined. Students may learn languages, math, history, economics, and the like in school, along with the theory underpinning their occupational area. But in some strong VET systems, aspects of general education are embedded in company training. For example, students may learn math and writing in applied forms on the job. As they progress in their learning, students may pass a series of assessments or demonstrations of competencies, skills, and knowledge. Final assessments may separate school learning and company learning so that the student receives two diplomas, or both may be assessed together. In either case, the employer takes part in the assessment of the student's occupational accomplishments. In many countries, the attainment of a qualification is required to practice the profession and so is a ticket to the job market.

To ease the burden on employers and to manage the collaboration between companies, schools, and young people, all countries have some form of intermediary organization or organizations. Generally organized by sector of the economy (construction, communications, commercial banking, transportation, social services), these organizations can have a wide variety of functions. Most important, they represent employer groups in creating qualifications, assessments, and curriculum. Many carry out aspects of training, such as providing orientation for apprentices or running short courses of interest to multiple employers in a sector. In some systems, they may execute contracts with trainees or apprentices and even hire them and send them out to companies. Many such organizations are also part of a tiered governance or steering system sending representatives of their sector to sit on national skills councils or to negotiate with labor unions.

The economics of such systems are complex, and training a young person in the workplace while she or he is also completing requirements for an upper secondary diploma is expensive. Nonetheless, even in very different financing models, the returns are worth the costs, both immediately and in forgone social costs for unemployment, social unrest, and the need for social security. Public entities, usually a combination of states or regions and the local and national governments, always pay for the in-school portion of VET. Apprentices and trainees receive training wages, usually starting at a low percentage of the entry level and increasing to parity or near it at the end of the years as a student, as they become fully productive. Some countries provide per-student subsidies for each student place in a company, while in other countries—notably in Germany and Switzerland—companies themselves support their apprentices. Other forms of government support include levies on nontraining companies to finance those that do train, tax breaks for those that train, subsidies to incentivize companies to take on challenging groups, and special incentives to train in sectors of the economy where jobs are open. Many countries also invest in the infrastructure for VET, including such costs as research and development, funding for intermediary organizations, and training of VET teachers and trainers.

While it is true that VET does not have the status of the academic, university pathway in most countries, it is increasingly popular and respected for a number of reasons. Technical training in such fields as engineering technology, IT, or tourism requires skills that are better learned in applied settings and respond to obvious needs in the economy. These fields are appealing to young people because they know the record-high percentages of students completing their apprenticeships or trainee stints are hired by the companies that train them, a major attraction in this economy. And in most, articulated pathways lead to higher education or *tertiary level*, as it is called in the international standard classification. For these reasons, at companies like Swisscom, profiled later in this book, it is not unusual to have seven thousand applications from fifteen- and sixteen-year-olds for eight hundred places in the company. Thus, with the downturn in the economy and more young people wanting to participate, the challenge to

VET everywhere is maintaining sufficient apprenticeships and internship openings to meet demand, and to identify a younger cohort of instructors since many VET teachers are reaching retirement age.

There is an additional reason that young people do well in VET, and
perhaps it is the most important one for a U.S. audience. The most intensive forms of workplace learning—apprenticeships and sustained internships—are especially effective in meeting the developmental needs
of young people. They provide a structure to support the transition
from adolescence to adulthood, now lacking for the majority of young
people in the United States who do not go to residential four-year colleges. Apprenticeships provide increasingly demanding responsibilities
and challenges in an intergenerational work setting that lends a structure to each day. Adult relationships are built on support and account-
ability, mentoring and supervision.

UNITED STATES AND "COLLEGE FOR ALL"

Whatever one concludes about the United States' average performance
in the transition to work, the United States is not average or middle-
of-the-road in the education strategy it is pursuing—college for all.
The United States is currently an outlier in focusing on postsecondary completion rather than on education having as its primary purpose
to help young people find a calling or vocation. The successes of other
countries and the paths they are pursuing raise the following questions:
will increasing attainment of postsecondary degrees produce the best
educational and labor market outcomes for young people and for our
economic prosperity? Should the United States be paying more attention to integrating work and learning, and providing guidance and
support not just to complete a credential, but to choose one of value
and get some work experience during late adolescence?

Some tantalizing recent data from the Georgetown Center on Education and the Workforce suggests that educators need to look closely
at the relation between education and career choice. The example: 22
percent of AA degree holders earn more than the median earnings of
BA holders, and 14 percent more than the median earnings of those
with graduate degrees—the reason has to do with the need for the

skills they have acquired, not the fact that they have completed a degree.[6] This data points in the direction that most other countries are pursuing.

Three trends stand out in contrast to the United States among the OECD countries studied:

- Countries that already have strong vocational education systems are strengthening them by adding more apprenticeship opportunities, retooling curriculum to better match labor market needs, adding high-tech postsecondary pathways, and engaging at-risk young people in integrated work and learning programs through "youth guarantees" and "mutual obligation" policies.

- Vocational education is promoted as the pathway of choice for the majority, with postsecondary options increasingly including traineeships; university education is designed for a small number of young people bound for research careers or law, medicine, and the like.

- A few countries (Korea, England) that have had a college-for-all strategy are rethinking it—adding more postsecondary career-oriented options with work-based learning requirements, and reinventing or expanding upper secondary pathways that include apprenticeships and training schemes in high-demand occupations.

ORGANIZATION OF THIS BOOK

The focus of this book is an age group—fifteen- to twenty-year-olds, those young people who between these years should be completing secondary education and getting launched into a career or further education. Its more specific focus is on all those young people in this age group who do not follow the path most valued—from high school to completion of an academic BA degree.

The chapters explore some key features of what I call strong VET systems, as defined above. I have tried to organize the book by anticipating the questions that thoughtful and knowledgeable U.S. readers have about vocational education in Europe and Australia—the systems that are best known here. Chapter 1 takes a hard look at the philosophical underpinnings of strong VET systems as well as at the currency that they yield for students—standardized and validated qualifications for a job articulated in the language of outcomes. It asks how countries can ensure that VET is broad and learning is for a calling, not a narrow trade, while at the same time assessing work readiness. It anticipates questions about whether VET sacrifices the values associated with liberal arts education in the United States.

Chapters 2 and 3 focus on the conundrum of employer engagement—a key aspect of VET that usually prompts readers in the United States to say, "It can't happen here." Chapter 2 asks questions about how similar countries do or do not develop strong VET systems, and why some are successful in engaging employers in educating and credentialing young people, while others are not. How do employers organize themselves to take on legally binding agreements with labor unions and educational institutions as well as contracts with sixteen-year-olds? What incentivizes firms (and unions) to take major responsibility with the government for the education and training of the next generation of workers? The following chapter zeros in on the structure of the strongest VET systems—those categorized as "state-directed" (but not state-run) systems characterized by a partnership of government, employers, unions, and schools. Because employer engagement seems so daunting when observed from afar, the chapter pays special attention to the structures that support employers and ease the burdens of being educators. These are various kinds of intermediary organizations that function as the "glue" between young people, employers, schools, and the state.

The final two chapters again attempt to anticipate questions of U.S. readers that intrigued me and about which there is little information: how teaching and learning actually take place in a work setting, and how strong VET countries adapt VET policies and practices to serve struggling young people and those at risk of school dropout and exclusion from the labor market.

The headline about pedagogy in the workplace is that it was so difficult to get a good picture of how this happens that I have included a personal journal from my visits to various apprenticeship sites to complement what I could glean from research and discussion. Readers will not be surprised to learn that all countries struggle to execute high-quality workplace learning. It must be—by reason of how work is organized and presented—problem based. Teaching algebra alone will not help students review credit applications, nor will teaching physics alone help them repair a truck. The difference, of course, from problem-based learning in schools is that problems do not have to be invented at work. Nonetheless, trainers must know how to explain problems. Students must learn how to think about problems and learn the vocabulary to use in solving them, and they must do so while listening to, respecting, and questioning experts. They must also be preparing for final broad assessments. So the pedagogy is different from and more challenging than getting a new employee started on the job.

As for students at risk of failure, countries do not expect that they will simply be absorbed into the VET system. For one thing, most employers did not sign up to be social workers; they are seeking and contracting with the highest-achieving young people in VET. So students in danger of being left behind are protected through social security, labor market activation policies requiring participation in school and work combinations, and guarantees issued to youth about their rights to work and training. When employers do take on "problem" students, they are usually incentivized to do so through extra stipends or other rewards. Nonetheless, as this chapter suggests, combinations of work and learning can be structured to stem dropout and to put the majority of young people on a pathway to productive adulthood.

THE CHOICE OF COUNTRIES TO PROFILE

One question that may puzzle readers is why I chose to profile Switzerland rather than Germany, which is usually held up as the best of the dual or apprenticeship systems. Or why I chose to profile Norway instead of Denmark, which has been the site of many U.S. visits to study that country's VET system. The answer is that I did not try to do a comprehensive overview of all work-based learning of any quality throughout the OECD countries. That would have been impossible. I tried to select examples from systems that would stretch U.S. thinking about occupational learning, as well as systems with structures that have aspects that might appeal to educators and employers

Tracking

Many readers will associate career and technical education in United States and European vocational education with tracking: students with the fewest social and economic resources end up in vocational programs that limit their future educational choices and career prospects. Concern about the potentially pernicious effects of early tracking continues to preoccupy the OECD countries. They keep data about and are sensitive to the relationship between parental education and income, and school results. The OECD, for example, compares countries on these factors, with greater variation within schools than between them, a signal that schools serving differing populations are achieving similar results.

Tracking takes two forms in the OECD countries: in Austria, Germany, Switzerland (most cantons), and the Netherlands, students choose or are placed into a vocational or academic pathway between the ages of ten and twelve. The Nordic countries and Australia have comprehensive schools through the end of lower secondary school, with everyone following the same curriculum. Then at age fifteen or sixteen, students and their families have a choice of a university or vocational pathway.

To deal with concerns about tracking, instead of pushing career preparation out of upper secondary schooling, so as not to perpetuate the social class differences that the practice can magnify, most countries have expanded VET from its earlier guild, handcraft, blue-collar identity so that white-collar occupations and those requiring sophisticated technical

in the United States. I delved into countries I had visited, and where there was sufficient data and research in English or French for me to feel confident that I could produce good minicases.

For example, arguably Switzerland has the best vocational education system in the world, but it is not well known, perhaps because Germany, a much larger country, has done more to export its system. Particularly interesting in Switzerland is that VET has considerable status there. In a study of the 2000 cohort of Swiss young people, VET was the choice of 42 percent of those who had attained the highest scores (4 and 5) on PISA. In addition, as evidence about choice rather than tracking, some 19 percent of middle scorers entered the academic track that leads to a university. See the box "Tracking." Germany still tracks learning are included. Thus, modern apprenticeships and traineeships, as they are often called to distinguish them from the traditional trade apprenticeships, are all about the use of high technology, cutting-edge business practices, engineering, media, and other twenty-first-century occupations.

A number of VET countries have built or are currently building attractive postsecondary linkages with upper secondary VET systems. This allows young people to move from the broad skills in a particular occupational pathway right into a technical diploma or management program at the postsecondary level, or return to complete higher education after some years of work beyond their apprenticeship. Indeed, countries have created whole new sets of tertiary institutions to provide technical and occupational training and skills to meet student and employer needs. So Switzerland, for example, has a VET/PET system—with PET standing for professional education and training—the pathway from VET to higher education. Many of these postsecondary pathways also have an internship or apprenticeship requirement. The rationale is that one can hardly move into a firm without having learned to apply school knowledge to the everyday problems in an occupation. The phrase often used to characterize this antitracking strategy is *no dead ends*.

Despite modernized VET systems, it is important to acknowledge that most academically gifted students do choose the university pathway, which carries greater prestige and requires admission to competitive upper secondary schools. In my work with various OECD countries, I have not met many parents among the officials with whom I have chatted whose children are in the vocational system.

students at an early age based on their academic records. Bob Schwartz, who was a member of the OECD *Learning for Jobs* team that visited Germany, describes the German dilemma, among other aspects of that VET system, in his personal reflections, also included in the book. (See the journal essay "The German Dual System.")

In regard to the choice of Norway, not only have I been fortunate enough to have worked on three OECD projects there, the country is the only one among the strong VET countries with a so-called two-plus-two system that may have some interest for the United States. Norway is also interesting because it is struggling with a dropout problem from VET and is making some modifications in the system to better integrate school and workplace learning. Finally, Australia and the

Netherlands, also profiled here, have attractive features—among them, strong youth policies, aggressive interventions to support vulnerable young people from failing in the labor market, and an array of inter-mediary organizations that provide the infrastructure for VET. They also have data and research in English, and I was able to spend time in Rotterdam with researchers, policy makers, and school people.

THEY'RE GOOD, WE'RE FAILING, OR VICE VERSA

This book will likely read as if most of what I highlight is better than what we do in the United States and is without immediate or long-term challenges for educators and employers. That is, of course, not the case. First, I relied on research and conversations for the country portraits, and while most policies and practice descriptions will appear to be meeting quality criteria, it is likely they would look more mixed on the ground. Second, I have tried to exemplify the VET systems where policy, goals, and purpose are admirable. The countries profiled support the growth and development of young people, take particu-lar steps to launch young people into the labor market so that they do not experience long periods of unemployment or drift, and respect the needs of employers and the economy. But that doesn't mean that they are universally successful. In Norway, a rich country with a thriving job market, some students give up VET and transfer into the univer-sity track or drift out of school into jobs that don't require a creden-tial. Australia is trying to raise the status of VET as well as to use it to improve the outcomes of its indigenous people who suffer severe and long-term impoverishment and exclusion. The Netherlands is strug-gling to simplify and perhaps shorten the path from upper secondary VET into vocational tertiary pathways so as to provide wider oppor-tunities. And in all these countries, vigilance is required to ensure that sufficient apprenticeship places are available in the current economy.

For the reasons noted above, this book tries not to take a "lessons from elsewhere" approach with a set of case-by-case studies of the sys-tems of other countries considered more successful than the United States. So how to situate this work? U.S. readers tend to think about non-U.S. systems for transitioning young people from school to what is nicely called in many OECD countries "the working life" in two ways, one positive and the other problematic: there are strong, enviable apprenticeship systems sponsored by employers in cooperation with the state and unions where work and learning are integrated and result in both an industry qualification and a job; and there is a tracking system with less academically gifted students selected into vocational training as early as age ten or twelve and certainly by fifteen. With tracking comes the replication of social class differences to a greater degree than in the United States, or at least theoretically.

In truth, apprenticeships and early tracking are simple labels for the complex picture of how countries outside the United States handle the transition from school to work. As I have noted, some countries with early tracking and strong apprenticeship systems now provide pathways to university degrees for those who desire them and have succeeded in keeping options open, including the possibility of changing sectors in the job market after training. And apprenticeship systems differ both within and across countries. Countries also use varieties of work-based learning that look more like the best of U.S. career-oriented high schools, providing a strong foundation in basic skills for everyone, and differentiating work preparation only in the final years of schooling (so between the ages of eighteen and nineteen), with work-based learning serving the purpose of a career introduction. In addition, in a number of countries, a discussion is under way much like that in the United States about the need for education or training beyond upper secondary career education. But if there's one strong, consistent argument that undergirds *Learning for Jobs* and this book, it is that workplace learning "has compelling attractions" both for young people and for employers; indeed, done well, it appears to be the best way for the majority of young people to prepare for the world of work.[7]

1

Qualifying for a Calling

The Philosophical Rationale for Vocational Education

To do productive work is a fundamental human need. Work supports families, promotes the well-being of communities, and ensures the health of the economy. Work attaches citizens to the public sphere. Work also helps individuals form strong identities and enables people to act in the world. Why would a society not want to support young people directly in finding good work and learning to do it well as insurance for their future prosperity and stability?

In the best work and learning systems—what I call strong VET systems—young people complete the portion of their education that is "all school" at around age fifteen or sixteen. As they mature from the later teenage years to about age twenty, they enter a period of "learning to work," which integrates school and work experience in a specific career area and ends with a nationally recognized qualification—generally their ticket to a decent job. By their early twenties, young people enter their careers, often transitioning seamlessly from integrated work and learning into full-time roles in their apprenticeship or internship companies. In the course of writing this book, I have become even more convinced of the benefits of such a system to young people, their families, communities, and society. I hope to convince U.S. policy makers, educators, and all those who care about the healthy development of young people to ask how the United States can create a system to realize similar benefits.

As outlined in the introduction, several essential factors make high-quality VET possible: a broad conception of vocation, a qualifications system that codifies agreements among occupational sectors (with government validation) as to what an entry-level worker needs to know and be able to do, employer engagement, and intermediary organizations that share the responsibility with employers for workplace learning. The contributions and commitments of employers and intermediaries are treated later on in this book. This chapter attempts to describe the philosophical rationale for VET in several countries, a rationale that contrasts with the purposes of career and technical education for young people in the United States. It also defines qualifications, the coin of the realm for understanding and certifying what educated adults know and are able to do. The chapter concludes with an explanation of how the European Community's attempt to establish cross-national qualifications is invigorating debate about how to define the outcomes for vocational learning.

The concept of calling or vocation underlies the way strong vocational education countries go about structuring the pathways for young people from schooling to work; thus understanding the concept is important to setting the stage for this book. The philosophical foundation for VET affects the nature and purpose of vocational education: vocational education exists not for career exploration purposes or to keep young people in school as in the United States—although that is its positive effect—but rather to support the development of teenagers as they transition from school into the world of work that will occupy and define their adult lives. The core around which broad learning is structured is an occupation chosen at around age sixteen and sometimes earlier. But strong VET countries place learning the specific skills needed for each occupation—to weld or solve banking problems or manage the IT system in a corporation—within a broad educational framework. Whatever the level of occupational education—whether auto mechanic, social worker, or computer programmer—young people are taught to approach their entrance into working life as a step on the way to an adulthood. Work in a company introduces the choices and responsibilities they will have at home and at work. Their period of practice in the workplace gives them increasing competence

24

and agency. Take Switzerland, Germany, Austria, the Netherlands, and Norway, where working at a paid occupation is viewed broadly as an aspect of active citizenship, and thus the education and training needed for work are seen as the joint responsibility of the government and the "social partners" (employers and labor unions).

One vivid way that economists describe such broadly construed career education is to say that the student has "property rights over their general training that increases their mobility."[1] Narrow training would make the young person of value to the company that mounted the training, but their skills would not be portable—not of much value to a firm unlike the one where she or he was trained. Broad training allows young people to market their qualifications to a range of employers, and incentivizes firms to compete for talent. To use a U.S. phrase that nicely characterizes the best of a broad education, the young person has the ability to "think for a living" in a variety of settings and to do so while applying her job-specific skills. In addition, if the young person "owns" broad skills, she is more likely a candidate for further education, whether at a university or through an advanced technical training program.

Along with calling or vocation, *qualification* is a key term in the VET lexicon and might be characterized as the linchpin of the system. The European Union (EU) has carefully defined the term *qualification* to distinguish the colloquial meaning of job requirements from the formal meaning. The colloquial definition of qualification is used to talk about skills, education, and work experience. In other words, qualifications are what in the United States make up the body of most job descriptions—what the ideal candidate should have. The EU defines qualification within a national qualifications system in a more precise way: "a qualification is the formal outcome (certificate, diploma, or title) of an assessment and validation process obtained when a competent body determines that an individual has achieved learning outcomes to given standards and/or possesses the necessary competence to do a job in a specific area of work."[2] A qualification confers official recognition of the value of learning outcomes in the labor market and in education and training. A qualification gives one an identity in the world of work. Strong VET countries have qualifications systems covering the majority of occupations and often suboccupations; in several, these are incorporated into a framework that standardizes and designates levels of competence.

Most U.S. readers would anticipate a tension between vocation or calling and qualifications. That is, often words like *competence, learning outcomes,* and *standards,* used in the definition above, signal a focus on discrete tasks and compartmentalized knowledge rather than a more holistic and thus humanistic concept. In countries with extensive VET systems, that is not the case. Qualifications are multidimensional, marrying systematic and contingent knowledge with social and personal qualities, which add up to how one "performs" in an occupation. There are qualifications of varying levels of specificity and varying emphases, covering a spectrum from specific skills to work processes to habits of mind suited to an occupation. For example, "attitudes" are an official element in the Netherlands' qualifications. As a Dutch researcher notes about tensions between job-specific and general skills, "characteristically for Dutch debates on VET, these tensions are *de facto* accepted by all stakeholders and seen as a consequence of the fact that three major stakeholders share responsibility for VET. The issue in many debates is not to deny the right of other parties to intervene, but to come up with compromises (for the time being), acceptable for all."[3]

Whatever the content of the qualification statement, the partners who develop and write such statements are cognizant of the challenge of joining the two key aspects of strong VET systems: broad education and work-specific skills. They recognize the tendency for the broadly construed qualities of a calling or vocation to devolve into narrow and instrumental skills that are easier to identify in a workplace, turn into an outcomes statement, and assess. Government and social partners, therefore, guard against this eventuality: in a number of countries, breadth is codified in law and is so deeply embedded in the culture that when collaborative partnerships form to write, revise, and validate qualifications, the broad notion of a calling is always present.

Currently, to respond to the force of rapid globalization, the European Community is engaged in attempting to harmonize qualifications systems across countries, thus engaging participating governments and their social partners in refining and stating clearly their approaches to qualifications. In so doing, they are raising important arguments for maintaining breadth and giving attention to processes as well as outcomes.

Countries that have historically had strong VET systems also have long had national qualifications. Countries building VET systems for the first time are developing qualifications systems and frameworks. The goal is to promote cross-country labor force mobility through a formal and public understanding that puts all qualifications into a single framework, with levels of equivalence spelled out in parallel with what the academic community is doing for academic higher education through the Bologna Process.[4] A serious question is whether a credible and extensive VET system can exist without qualifications; see the box "'Qualifications' in the United States" for a brief summary of standardized career credentials in the United States.

DIFFERENT VET STRUCTURES, SIMILAR RATIONALES

The brief profiles of varied VET systems below demonstrate the ways that countries conceptualize the aims of VET: integrating skills, competencies, and knowledge; attending to problem solving and the application of learning; and ensuring that learning is broadly contextualized. The systems profiled are Germany and Switzerland, which provide upper secondary vocational learning largely through apprenticeships; the Netherlands, which is primarily school based, with varying amounts of workplace experience; and Norway and Australia. The latter two countries separate their school-based and workplace components. Norway provides two years of school followed by two years of apprenticeship, while Australia's extensive qualifications system is undergirded by outcomes-based curricula, called training packages, which are delivered by a variety of providers. France is the final example. While the education system is struggling to deliver what it promises in VET, the nation's rationale, encapsulated in *formation*, a word with no English equivalent but having a resonance of development of the whole person. In each case, I sketch out the philosophical rationale with attention to the way breadth of study is explained and institutionalized, with some examples of how qualifications for specific occupations are described.

"Qualifications" in the United States

In the United States, qualifications do exist in some fields, but they are not the coin of the realm in most. The recent focus on raising the U.S. rate of postsecondary completion has resulted in attention to several long-neglected career credentials: certificates, licenses, and certifications.

Certificates
Educational institutions award certificates to indicate completion of a program of study that does not culminate in a degree. Criteria vary widely among institutions—even within the same higher education system or state. Certificates are not the same as certifications. Some certificates, like medical coding, have currency nationally; students take a standardized exam. Others, like international business, an offering at Bunker Hill Community College in my home city of Boston, gather together a set of courses from the AAS degree of the same title, but are not standardized across the state or country.

Certifications
Certifications are closer to qualifications than certificates are in that they are awarded by a third party, often a professional organization. A standard-setting entity assesses the applicant's competence against standards in a particular occupational area. Cisco Systems Networking Specialists and other Cisco certifications are likely the best known. Professional organizations in such fields as aviation, construction, technology, and health care issue certifications.

Germanic Countries

VET in the Germanic countries did not just naturally emerge in its current form from the old trades. It had a founding education-theorist father, Georg Kerschensteiner, born in 1854. Kerschensteiner believed that neither school nor apprenticeship alone would develop a young person's moral, social, and occupational sensibilities and competence. He sought to bridge the pragmatic and the humanistic. With a tradition of educating the majority of adolescents in company-based apprenticeships, the Germanic countries (Austria, Germany, and Switzerland) define the vocational principle as *Berufskonzept*, which is derived from the German word *ruf*, meaning "calling." *Beruf* signifies "a body of systematically related theoretical knowledge (*Wissen*) and a set of practical

Licenses

Licenses are the credential most similar to qualifications in that they serve as the sole ticket of admission to an occupation; one cannot practice without one. Earning a license to practice usually requires examination by a licensing board of experienced practitioners in the same field. It frequently requires that the applicant complete a prescribed course of study and present a certificate or degree attesting to successful completion of that program. Virtually all health-care licensing and certification authorities require completion of specific, institutionally based education programs.[a] Licensure differs from certification in that it is a legal requirement, and licensing boards are subject to public oversight, usually by state or local government authorities. However, licensing standards and procedures differ from one state to another and thus are not completely portable.[b]

If the United States were to get serious about developing a national qualifications system accompanied by workplace training, one place to start would be with certifications and licenses. These credentials already have standards, assessments, and requirements for the completion of a practicum, clinical training, or an internship, as well as specified hours and tasks to be learned.

[a] Brian Bosworth, *Certificates Count: An Analysis of Sub-Baccalaureate Certificates* (Washington, DC: Complete College America, 2010), 6.
[b] Ibid., ii.

skills (*Konnen*) as well as the social identity of the person who has acquired these. Achievement of such an identity is certified by a diploma upon passing an examination and is on this basis recognized legally and without question by all employers and goes together with a particular status and wage grade."[5]

The official aims of the *Berufschule*, or vocational schooling, in Germany include three *Kompetenze*, the word for "competencies":

- *Fachkompetenz:* the disposition and ability, on the basis of expert knowledge and know-how, to solve tasks and problems purposefully, appropriately, and autonomously by using the right methods.

- *Personalkompetenz:* the disposition and ability to be clear about, review, and assess opportunities to develop demands and restrictions imposed by family, occupation, and the public; to fulfill one's own potential as well as to make and develop life plans. It encompasses personal qualities such as autonomy, critical faculties, self-confidence, reliability, a sense of responsibility and duty, and, in particular, development of moral concepts and self-determined commitment to moral values.

- *Sozialkompetenz:* the disposition and ability to live and create social relations, to realize and understand devotion and tension as well as communicate and engage with others rationally and responsibly, and to develop social responsibility and solidarity.[6]

The following example is illustrative of the *Beruf* of *Spezialtiefbauer*—civil engineering specialists—in the German construction industry, described as "carrying out tasks on the basis of technical information and instruction, both independently and in cooperation with others. They plan their work in cooperation with others on site, set up construction sites, determine the individual work steps required and take the measures required for health and safety at work and to protect the environment. They check their work for defects, measure the quantities done and hand over the site after clearing up."[7]

In the Germanic systems, academic and vocational learning are integrated. Austrian, German, and Swiss students learn mathematics in the course of their apprenticeships, not in separate math classes; literacy skills are embedded as well. Students typically spend one or two days per week in school doing academic and theoretical work. In Switzerland, VET students learn first and second national languages (so German or Italian, if you live in French Switzerland), a third language, history, economics, math, and electives. Switzerland also requires special training for teachers who provide instruction in the general subjects for VET students so that they can contextualize the disciplines within the world of work.

In a Germanic context, then, a *Qualifikation* certifies an ability (*Fähigkeit*) and represents a socially recognized and legally binding guarantee that someone possesses certain kinds of knowledge (propositional, practical, or both) associated with a specific *Beruf*.[8]

The Netherlands

The Dutch VET system is multifaceted, with early tracking (eighth grade) and many decision points along the way. Once in VET, students can choose the level of their learning, their career goals, and how much of their training will take place in school and how much in the workplace. The majority of students are in school-based VET, with around 60 percent of their time in a workplace. Like the Germanic countries, the Dutch have a broad concept of occupation made up of knowledge, skills, and attitudes. The Dutch are quite clear that they reject what they define as the Anglo-Saxon definition of competence, which requires "a rigid backward mapping approach, in which the state of the art on the shop floor is the starting point for the definition of occupational competencies, leading to routinized job descriptions."[9] As Anneke Westerhuis, a prominent Dutch VET researcher, notes, national qualifications developed in this way "are mechanistic, reductionist and denying the importance of human agency in processes of learning.[10] She goes on to describe the Dutch approach as "integrative": "In VET, competence is understood as the integration of abilities required to cope with complex tasks. What does work demand from a person? In answering this question, Dutch researchers tend to cover a wide area of human behavior in their definition of competences in terms of knowing, wanting, being and being able."[11]

Referring to the Germanic notion of competence, Westerhuis associates it with the German word for "performing" (*handelende*). "This crucial concept can be understood as '*handlungsfähig* behavior;' somebody's behavior will demonstrate, in an occupational context, whether or not he or she masters the necessary skills and knowledge and addresses people with an appropriate attitude (as defined by the social codes of the professional community)."[12]

VET is by statute required to prepare students for a lifetime career, lifelong learning, and citizenship, and not for a single job or position. Underscoring the importance of general education, the Netherlands has articulated its nonvocational attainment targets in an official document, *Leren, loopbaan en burgerschap* ("Learning, career and citizenship"), which is an integral part of all new qualification descriptions.

Specific language in a related document declares that "VET should address a student as a complete person, having to learn how to behave in occupational contexts as well as in society."[13] While the employment system is driven by qualifications that cover most occupations, the breadth and scope of these qualifications are the result of negotiations between the state, the schools, and the social partners—actually sector-based national committees, which take the lead in producing the qualifications. The government exercises quality control by validating and accrediting each set of qualifications that becomes part of the National VET Qualifications Framework.

Norway

With their egalitarian social values and their focus on equity and inclusion, the Nordic countries have universal education with a single curriculum through lower secondary school or to about age fifteen. Among the Nordic countries, Norway is the only country with a "two-plus-two" apprenticeship system serving all VET students—two years of upper secondary school followed by two years of apprenticeship. The other countries launch VET from schools with periods of varying length to try out and ultimately pursue various career options.

The rationale for VET is not as clearly articulated in Norway as in the Germanic countries. However, it is generally construed as encompassing broad competencies needed for entrance into working life, and as preparation for learning that is expected to continue during the entire life span. The phrase *working life* itself suggests that Norwegians recognize the multidimensionality of work not as a narrow set of skills, but as a broad identity necessary for productive adulthood. Norway shares with other Nordic countries a relaxed view of the schedule for completing schooling, perhaps because of its strong and varied options for lifelong learning, and the high participation rates in formal and informal learning by adults of all ages, all of which underscore a commitment to depth as well as breadth.

Students study common core subjects for 30 percent of their time during their first year of VET and 20 percent during their second year, with an emphasis on Norwegian, English, math, and economics. They devote 50 percent of their time to their vocational area. Each year includes an individually designed in-depth study project, as well as short-term experiences in their chosen enterprise area. This short-term internship also serves to introduce students to companies where they might choose to apply for an apprenticeship. Like much in Norway, unions, industries, schools, and the state operate in a regulated partnership under principles of equality and freedom of choice set out by Parliament. Vocational education is considered one with general education and is regulated by the same acts.

Australia

Australia has a thriving VET sector, with about 60 percent of eleventh- and twelfth-year students participating in what is called "VET in schools"; of participating students, about 40 percent are in workplace apprenticeships outside of school. VET students get their general education in school; they leave school to work in blocks of time of a day, or a week, or to study online. For high school–age students, schools offer industry-based units of competency that combine general and vocational studies with practical business and industry experience. They are designed in a sequence, allowing students to move steadily from one qualification to the next. Units of competency may be mixed and matched as long as they meet the requirements of the qualification. Undertaking industry-based training while at school can also lead to a dual qualification, the Senior Secondary Certificate of Education, and credits toward a vocational certificate, diploma, or degree qualifications.

In Australia, all statements about the purposes of VET include reference to lifelong learning, broad knowledge and skills, and the cultivation of habits of mind and attitudes that lead toward success at work and in one's community. To signal the importance of calling or vocation in the nation's philosophy, schools explicitly define VET as important for every student. For example, the Senior Secondary Certificate of Education that marks the completion of academic secondary education for everyone is defined as having the following learning outcomes: "knowledge, skills and understanding required as a basic preparation for life in the community, work and further study. These are developed through studies that may include academic disciplines, *vocational education and training* [emphasis mine], and community based learning."[14]

With an outcomes-based system that is agnostic about the sources of learning, the Australian Qualifications Framework (a quasi-legal document) defines the outcomes for each level of education, with one set of outcomes for academic areas and another for vocational achievement, all the way through to a graduate vocational diploma or doctorate. At Level III in VET, which is below the vocational diploma and so of midlevel in challenge, characteristics of learning outcomes include the following:

- Performance of a broad range of skilled applications, including requirements to evaluate and analyze current practices, develop new criteria and procedures for performing current practices, and provide some leadership and guidance to others in the application and planning of the skills.

- Breadth, depth, and complexity of knowledge and competencies, covering a broad range of varied activities or applications in a wider variety of contexts, most of which are complex and nonroutine.

- Leadership and guidance, involving when organizing activities of self and others as well as contributing to technical solutions of a nonroutine or contingency nature; applications involving responsibility for, and limited organization of, others.[15]

The recruitment information from Qantas, Australia's international airline (see box, "Quantas"), describes for young people fifteen years old and beyond the requirements to join the engineering apprenticeship program and the structure and qualifications offered in the training program, followed by the career development options when moving from entry level to becoming a management team member in the engineering field.

France

With academic knowledge held in highest regard, France educates its VET students in school, with limited experience in the workplace or apprenticeships. In France, VET serves only about 24 percent of students, most of them with low to mediocre skills. Nonetheless, France and other francophone countries have an expansive notion of "occupation," with an emphasis on the theoretical aspects. France is currently

Qantas: Success from the ground up

Requirements

Qantas has minimum entry level requirements that need to be considered before making your application to join the Qantas Engineering Apprenticeship program:

Essential Requirements

You can apply for one trade in one location (exceptions may apply from time to time);

- You must be an Australian Citizen or Permanent Resident;
- New Zealand Citizens with a minimum of 6 months residency in Australia may apply for Sydney and Brisbane based Trades only;
- You must be minimum of 15 years of age or older at time of employment (January 2012);
- Have completed a minimum of Year 10 or equivalent;
- Pass a Federal Police Criminal History Check; and
- Pass a Pre-employment Medical Examination.
- Brisbane Aircraft Trades (Avionics, Mechancial or Structures) are ONLY available to candidates who have successfully completed or will have completed an Aero Skills Pre-Vocational Course at the time of employment with one of the following institutions.
- Aviation Australia (Brisbane/Cairns)
- ATAE
- QLD Institute for Aviation Engineering

Brisbane Non Aircraft Trades, when available, are open to all candidates meeting the above essential requirements.

Please keep in mind that this is an entry level apprenticeship program. If you currently hold a recognised trade certificate or tertiary qualification, please be aware that our Apprenticeship consists of a nominal 4 year TAFE and work training period and that this option may not be the right one for you.

Source: http://www.careers.qantas.com.au/Apprentices/Requirements.aspx

Training

An apprenticeship will offer you the ability to work for a world-class organization while undertaking training to achieve a nationally recognized qualification in the Aerospace Industry.

- Apprentices attend the applicable TAFE College and receive instruction in the theoretical aspects of the trade.

(continued)

Qantas: Success from the ground up *(continued)*

- TAFE attendance can be either one day per week or in a block release pattern of days or weeks in succession.
- You are paid whilst attending TAFE.
- Apprentices are moved through the Engineering business into areas applicable to the relevant trade to be undertaken.
- Apprentices will undertake practical training developing the required practical skills and knowledge required to be granted an industry recognized qualification.
- During the practical training at the workplace you may be required to work shift work.

Future Career Development

Once your comprehensive training and apprenticeship is complete, you will be exposed to a diverse range of career and development options throughout Qantas Engineering and the greater Qantas Group. Some areas that may interest you are:

- Training to become a Licensed Aircraft Maintenance Engineer (LAME)
- Further your training through the Graduate Trainee Program to become a Professional Engineer
- Ascend through the ranks to become a Maintenance Supervisor
- Become a part of the Management Team in our Engineering Business
- Progress your career throughout the Qantas Group

Source: Adapted from http://careers.qantas.com/au/Apprentices/Requirements.aspx.

attempting to build stronger apprenticeship opportunities since youth unemployment is very high, and apprenticeship is thought to ease the transition into permanent employment.

In France, the term for VET is *formation professionelle*. This is a much broader concept than "training" and has the meaning of human being, citizen, and producer, the same three concepts for academic formation. In the same spirit as the German *Beruf*, the three component parts include:[16]

- To know (*savoir*)—technical competencies, the theoretical and systematic technical knowledge shaped to the discipline underlying the occupation

- To know how (*savoir-faire*)—operational competencies, the application of knowledge and experience to a concrete work problem or situation

- To know how to act or behave (*savoir-être*)—social competencies, such as the ability or capacity to act autonomously within a hierarchy, to work in a team, to communicate well with others[17]

Formation professionelle, or professional education, delivered in *lycees professionelles* is a recent development in France. The *baccalaureate professionelle* was introduced in 1985; it was established to provide vocational qualifications along with academic ones, so all baccalaureate candidates, whether academic or professional, sit for the same national public academic examination.

CROSS-BORDER QUALIFICATIONS

As noted, many countries already have very sophisticated systems for supporting young people in the attainment of nationally recognized qualifications, and a number of countries are engaged in refining or developing such standardized occupational qualifications—what students earn as a result of successful assessment at the end of upper secondary school. This is the trusted currency graduates bring to employers within their own countries when they go looking for a job. But each country's system is idiosyncratic—developed out of particular traditions and cultures. In an increasingly globalized world, Europe must function as an integrated economic community in many situations. Country borders present barriers to trade, employment, and innovation and creativity.

Beginning in 2000 with the Lisbon strategy for economic modernization, the European Commission has been working to increase the "transparency, comparability, transferability and recognition of qualifications" across the member countries.[18] A later development than the Bologna Process, which harmonizes higher education qualifications across twenty-seven member countries, the European Qualifications Framework (EQF) built on its successes. The basis for European cooperation in VET was laid out in the Copenhagen Declaration, which was endorsed in November 2002 by the education ministers of thirty-one

European countries, social partners, and the European Commission. The three goals are:

- Improving the quality and effectiveness of education and training systems in the European Union
- Facilitating the access of all to education and training systems
- Opening up education and training systems to the wider world

The framework comprises descriptors for lifelong learning from upper secondary through advanced training and education. (The Bologna Process fits within the EQF.)[19]

Sometimes described as a *transnational meta framework*, the qualifications framework sets out eight levels of knowledge, skills, and competence, ranging from those achieved at the end of upper secondary school through the highest level of vocational or professional training.[20] The three categories that make up qualifications—knowledge, skills, and competence—are derived from a compromise agreement based on the three distinct but overlapping philosophies and "cultures" of vocational education described in the section "Different VET Structures, Similar Rationales" above: the German-speaking countries' differentiation between *Fachkompetenz*, *Personalkompetenz*, and *Sozialkompetenz*; the French distinctions between *savoir*, *savoir-faire*, and *savoir-être*; and the English-speaking countries' distinctions between *cognitive competence*, *functional competence*, and *social competence*.

The key words here are *assessment*, meaning a process to establish the degree to which an individual has the knowledge, skills, and competences required; *validation*, meaning that the assessment is established against a public, tested standard separated from assessment and involving multiple stakeholders who have reached consensus that the outcomes are appropriate; and *recognition*, meaning that an awarding or regulatory body recognized as competent attests officially to the achievement of the learning required. A qualification confers official recognition of the value of learning outcomes in the labor market and in education and training. A qualification can be a legal entitlement to practice a trade.[21]

Perhaps most interesting is that for the first time in Europe, knowledge, skills, and competences are divorced from duration of education or particular degree or educational program. Thus, it would be possible for students earning qualifications in construction, IT networking, and physics all to achieve Level 5 (which corresponds to higher education, short cycle in the Bologna Process, despite the different mixes of theoretical, academic, hands-on, and applied knowledge in these fields). In other words, expertise is pegged to the specific occupation, with the underlying assumption that high levels of expertise can be achieved in all fields, however different the knowledge, skills, and competences required.[22] In 2008, 1.6 million résumés were generated.

In Level 5, for example, knowledge outcomes are comprehensive, specialized, factual, and theoretical knowledge within a field of work or study and an awareness of the boundaries of that knowledge. Skills outcomes are a comprehensive range of cognitive and practical skills required to develop creative solutions to abstract problems. Competences focus on autonomy and responsibility, including exercising management and supervision in contexts of work or study activities where there is unpredictable change, and reviewing and developing performance of self and others. Numerous pilot projects in specific occupations are under way, focusing on regions where cross-border mobility is significant, economic sectors are being internationalized (the automobile industry, for example), and small business sectors need multiskilled workers. Involving social partners, institutions, and employers, the specific occupations include a range from hairdressing and floristry to aeronautics, chemistry, live performing arts, and automation.[23]

One reason for the press to develop the EQF is that across Europe in the European Economic Area (EEA), governments want to remove barriers to cross-border mobility of workers. Such promotion of mobility has several purposes. First, cross-border mobility supports the principle of free movement of peoples—a cherished and hard-won European right enshrined in the 1995 Schengen Agreement, which abolished controls at the internal borders between the signatories, harmonized controls at the external frontiers, and introduced a common policy on short-stay visas for third-country nationals. Over 400 million people live in the Schengen area, which covers twenty-two EU member states, plus Iceland, Norway, and Switzerland, and many have reason to cross borders on business.[24]

Second, job vacancies are high in some countries and low in others. Greater cross-border mobility might lower unemployment rates if it were easier for citizens to cross borders to work, and if their qualifications were easily translatable from one education system to another.

Third, the EQF builds *zones of mutual trust*, which means that across borders employers and educators are able to "believe in" the credentials presented by job applicants trained outside of the hiring country. For example, some 900,000 European workers commute across borders every day for work and must negotiate different sets of expectations and qualifications. Many workers want to cross borders to improve their life chances and career opportunities, bringing with them certified qualifications—both vocational and academic—that would be best presented in a harmonized European framework.[25]

Finally, transparency is also important for quality production. For example, one of a set of pilot projects undertaken by the European Credit System for Vocational Education and Training (ECVET) attempts to harmonize qualifications in the European aeronautic and space industry. (See the box "Cross-National Qualifications.") The rationale for such a project—which is led by Germany, with the participation of France, Spain, and England—is that parts for a single plane are made in multiple countries, and the producers must have transparent qualifications in order to ensure the quality and compatibility of each assembled part.

The European Commission is developing additional components to support the European Qualifications Framework: Europass, an ECVET, and the European Quality Assurance Reference Framework for VET. Europass is a Web-based tool consisting of five documents: a standardized curriculum vitae that can be completed in twenty-six languages and includes not just education but informal learning as well, a language passport (a template for describing languages mastered and levels of competency), and three documents released to citizens who have achieved prespecified learning outcomes. One of these, the Certificate Supplement, describes the content of VET certificates downloadable from national inventories.

Cross-National Qualifications: Aeronautics Sector

Qualifications in the aeronautics sector are characterized by:

- The existence of European standards regarding qualifications of certain professions in this industry (namely regarding maintenance);
- The fact that aeronautic products for a single airplane are produced in different countries across Europe and have to meet the same quality criteria;
- Constant changes of work processes and materials used.

This high-tech professional sector therefore requires the establishment of a common language and strong transnational cooperation in order to ensure the quality of the final product.

The work of the AEROVET project is based on the outcomes of the AERONET pilot project (www.pilot-aero.net). AERONET aimed at acquiring in-depth knowledge of qualifications in the four partner countries in the aeronautic sector. It developed in-depth understanding of specific training regulations in the countries concerned and resulted in a repertory of typical professional tasks (TPTs) to cover the work of all aircraft construction professionals across Europe.

The AEROVET project will further develop the repertory of Typical Professional Tasks (TPTs) to cover the profession of aircraft maintenance staff. On the basis of TPTs, learning outcomes and units of learning outcomes will be developed. The formulation of the units will also have to take into account some normative requirements in the aerospace industry.

The AEROVET project will also explore the links with ECTS, as some of the qualifications concerned are awarded by higher education institutions using ECTS.

The project outcomes will be tested during three-month transnational exchanges of trainees within Airbus. Whilst such exchanges already exist, the learning outcomes of students who participate in them will this time be recognized.

Source: ECVET Bulletin. issue 1, 2009, http://www.ecvet-projects.eu.

Whether the attempt to create and broadly implement a voluntary European Qualifications Framework is successful or not—and success is by no means ensured—it has prompted countries to enter into discussion of their own conceptions of qualifications and has invigorated cross-national debate. It also has raised critical questions about process versus outcomes designs for VET. For example, although the Germanic systems have the best-known and most highly developed apprenticeship systems, they do not fuse easily with the EQF because they have been historically process based rather than outcomes based. In addition, there are questions about the utility of standardized qualifications in the labor market—countries differ in the degree to which employers judge potential employees by their formal qualifications, as opposed to experience, personal qualities, reputation of schools in which they are trained, and self-presentation. That is, while the aim of the EQF is to construct a "trusted currency" across borders, the process is starting with building within-border credibility.

CONCLUSION

One clear strength of higher education in the United States is liberal education, described by one of its champions as "a philosophy of education that empowers individuals with broad knowledge and transferable skills, and a strong sense of value, ethics, and civic engagement. Characterized by challenging encounters with important issues, [liberal education] is more a way of studying than a specific course or field of study."[26] The foundation for liberal education is the high school curriculum organized by traditional academic disciplines. Many U.S. educators object to learning for jobs because they fear that students would have to give up the broad introduction to culture that is intended to lead to civic engagement and lifelong learning. They fear that liberal education would be sacrificed to narrow, instrumental skills training. But as noted above, other countries do manage to integrate successfully certain, though not all, aspects of the liberal education approach into learning for work, rather than either keeping the two separate or insisting somewhat disingenuously that preparing for future work is not what true education is about. In addition, many of the countries mentioned have strong and thriving cultural institutions supported by government, rich arts communities, and substantial state-supported and informal participation in lifelong learning activities that provide some of the opportunities of liberal education.

Given the high secondary completion rates of countries using the VET strategy and their greater success than the United States in keeping youth unemployment low, and in moving cohorts of qualified young workers into the labor market with recognized skills, the United States might emulate countries that see learning to work not as opposed to a broad education but as an essential aspect of it.

2

Employer Engagement

Good for the Bottom Line,
Good for Young People

One of the most important elements of a strong VET system is a deep commitment from a country's employers. As noted in the previous chapter, employers play a major role, along with the government, in developing and maintaining effective VET programs. Companies not only open their doors each year to thousands of young people and teach them how to succeed in the world of work; they also apply their expertise to help design occupational qualifications, curriculum, and assessments used systemwide. All VET countries involve the business sector to a much greater degree than does the United States, where the culture does not place the same priority on job education and training for youth in the workplace. But even among OECD members where significant numbers of young people participate in vocational education, the amount and shape of employer engagement varies: in 2009, more than half of Australian employers reported having used the VET system in the previous twelve months; they had jobs requiring a VET qualification, employed an apprentice or trainee, or had staff that undertook nationally recognized training.[1] About 23 percent of employers in Germany and 30 percent in Switzerland train apprentices in their workplaces, a figure that has been relatively stable for some years.[2]

Why do some countries attract many companies to assist in educating and credentialing young people, while others do not? What are the benefits of engagement to employers? What are the barriers? What are the costs? In pragmatic terms, what incentivizes firms to share responsibility with the government for the education and training of the next generation of workers? This chapter explores these fundamental questions about the role of employers in VET systems.

BENEFITS

Extensive research literature documents the benefits of apprenticeships and workplace learning that characterize VET as "superior to full-time schools."[3] The evidence shows these benefits accrue to participating employers, as well as to the young people in training and to society as a whole. Researchers highlight three major advantages: "(a) the cognitive and motivational effects of integrating theory and practice in skill learning; (b) a closer correspondence between the content of skills and the requirements of actual production systems; and (c) increased youth employment rates, and better school-to-work transitions in general."[4]

For employers, one of the biggest benefits is the ability to hire entry-level youths who can reasonably quickly become productive workers, though technically they are learning to work. For a lower cost because the young people are paid as students, not regular entry-level employees, businesses build a young workforce capable of making valuable contributions to the enterprise. Organizations easily can ensure that training meets their specific needs. Unions also benefit from apprenticeship training, in that they have a say both in the setting of training wages for young people and in negotiating adult worker wage growth, which will be higher for trained employees than for those without training.[5]

Research suggests that this approach to job training and career preparation is more cost-effective than the usual U.S. route. Over the long run, it is less expensive for a company to partner with the public education system, labor unions, and business organizations to shape young people for full-time, regular employment while still in secondary school, than to undertake the U.S. alternative: hire on the basis of level of schooling completed, major field of study, and personal characteristics, and then provide the job-specific training needed. For entry-level jobs that demand few skills, U.S. employers often have little to go on in hiring a young person. This generates a wasteful cycle of hiring, trying out employees to see how quickly they can learn, and then firing slow learners to replace them with new, untried recruits. Employers providing substantial internships and apprenticeships have the opportunity to screen workers over a long period—at least six months and up to four years—before deciding whether to offer full, regular employment.

In addition, a robust apprenticeship system is associated with broader employer engagement with schooling and training of adolescents, in general. In other words, if employers take on apprentices, they not only will be engaged in the day-to-day education of their young employees but also will have a bigger stake in government policy regarding education and training of their country's youth—not just in qualifications, assessments, and curriculum for career education. They will be more engaged and more valuable corporate citizens. Given that training young people is a highly visible expression of corporate citizenship, participants also are likely to get a nice public relations bump from their involvement.

In an article in its November 2009 *Sustainability Newsletter* about its seven thousand apprentices, the German auto manufacturer Daimler rightly takes credit for increasing the number of slots so as to help stem youth unemployment in the current economic crisis. The following is excerpted from Daimler's *Sustainability Newsletter:*

> The most popular technical vocations are automotive mechatronic engineer and manufacturing mechanic. Business administrators are at the top of the list in the commercial sector. . . . At the University of Cooperative Education, Daimler offers a total of eleven courses of study in the technical and administrative fields. . . . The proportion of female trainees in the industrial and technical fields reached last year's level of around eleven percent, while some 30 percent of students at the University of Cooperative Education are women. Daimler's Human Resources Board member Wilfred Porth emphasized the great significance given to vocational training in times of crisis. "We offer young people a vocational perspective, and this year too we are providing training above and beyond our own requirements," said Porth. "With our commitment to training we are living up to our social responsibility, as well as securing expertise for our talented youngsters and thus ensuring our entrepreneurial success.

As part of the Pact for Training Future Specialists, Daimler also gives young people who have not been able to secure an apprenticeship the opportunity to undergo vocational pre-qualifications at German production and sales sites.[6]

Workplace learning also has numerous indirect benefits for employers. Apprenticeship training leads to substantially higher upper secondary completion rates and lower youth unemployment than in nonapprenticeship countries. Countries with apprenticeships and strong school-based VET with a work component also have fewer social costs, such as income and social services benefits for the unemployed, and costs of crime, drug abuse, and other ills associated with unemployment. This benefits employers in lower taxes.

My observations in visiting with apprentices in a number of OECD study sites underscore the ways in which apprenticeships give students as young as sixteen a sense of purpose and well-being, as well as wages that lend them an age-appropriate independence as they become adults. A number of the young people with whom I spoke were mediocre students at fifteen, but with some firm training completed, they now had aspirations not just for a career but for higher education, a goal supported by their employers. (See my journal essay in this volume, "Ordinary Teenagers, Extraordinary Results.")

VARIATIONS IN EMPLOYER ENGAGEMENT

Despite its many benefits, employer engagement in job training for youth is far from universal. The United States is not the only developed country that does not have a sustainable, extensive work-based learning system for young people. Neither has Sweden nor England nor France nor Korea—to name a few countries with a high regard for education and a wide variety of social and economic institutions.

Consider Sweden: Sweden is similar to other Nordic countries in the structure of its primary and secondary education system, in its union membership covering a majority of the workforce, and in its strong public policy focus on social equality. However, Sweden has a school-based vocational education system, with limited and informal employer participation.[7] Meanwhile, its Nordic neighbors Denmark, Norway, and Finland each engage employers to various but significant extents in educating the youth population in the workplace, and have a formal legal structure for doing so.

Students in the Swedish VET system are entitled to a fifteen-week internship during their three years of vocational upper secondary school, but it is not uniformly made available. In the *Learning for Jobs* review of Sweden in 2007 of which I was a part, we advocated for making apprenticeship and other work-based learning opportunities widely available and increasing employer engagement. Yet government ministry officials, union representatives, and educators shook their heads and said, essentially, we appreciate how important this is, but it won't happen here: "We tried it in the late '90s and it failed." Companies believe that since they pay high taxes and education enjoys strong financial support, business should reap the benefits of their financial contributions by having schools prepare young people for careers. But taxes are high in other Nordic countries, as well; nonetheless, their governments subsidize workplaces for student learning, and Sweden's could do so, too. So explanations of why the systems have differed are hard to find.

Recently, however, Swedish thinking about career training apparently has started to evolve. Several years after the *Learning for Jobs* review, Sweden is taking up the OECD's recommendation to implement a pilot apprenticeship program that requires that more than 50 percent of the total amount of vocational education be in the workplace.[8]

The variations between countries within the British Commonwealth make another interesting case in point: Australia and England share characteristics in their education systems generally, but differ in their commitment to workplace training for young people. Australia has a strong and increasingly popular apprenticeship system at both the secondary and postsecondary levels, with deep employer leadership, while England is struggling to rebuild an apprenticeship system from a weak base. The Australian VET system is underpinned by a commitment to competency-based learning, with qualifications defined by Australian industry, and a robust roster of registered training organizations that supplement and support company programs. VET competencies and qualifications cover around 80 percent of occupations.

England, by contrast, has had a serious decline in apprenticeships and never had a strong VET system, even thirty years ago. Similar to the United States, England has a socioeconomically bifurcated system in which the "haves" go on to university and good jobs, while the "have-nots" languish without quality credentials, decent jobs, or family-sustaining wages. Only 76 percent of twenty-five- to thirty-four-year-olds had an upper secondary education in 2006, below the OECD average.[9] To the degree that apprenticeships exist in England, they tend to go to people older than nineteen. In 2006–2007, only 7 percent of students between ages sixteen and eighteen were in an apprenticeship.[10] Employers do not think of apprentices as students, but rather as employees, who require training for their specific jobs.

England now faces a challenge in trying to revive apprenticeship for the twenty-first century—a strategy the Cameron government has identified as a key policy lever in the face of declining youth employment in the financial crisis. With a new conservative government dramatically remaking education policy, England has just published a book-length *Review of Vocational Education* commissioned by the secretary for education and written by Oxford professor Alison Wolf, hence called "the Wolf report." Echoing concerns in the United States about low-quality career education, the Wolf report reviles the waste in the many dead-end credentials of English VET, which result in large numbers of young people who "'churn,' moving between qualifications that provide little scope for progression, and unsatisfactory, often short-term employment or periods of unemployment." The report goes on to say that their school-earned qualifications are of such low quality that they "would have been substantially better off if they had not taken them, and been employed instead . . . The result is that about one third of young people leave school without evidence of useful skills." The report calls for more apprenticeships and other work-based learning.[11]

But this will prove challenging, indeed. A theme of the review is government frustration that England lacks a strategy to engage employers as educators—in large measure because of a qualifications system that employers manage through sector skills councils without government standardization or quality control. The result is that

England historically has had an inordinate focus on specific job skills and has never articulated broad vocational principles on the order of those in the Germanic countries.

BARRIERS

Given the many benefits of workplace learning for young people, it would be useful to explain why some countries have succeeded in establishing strong and successful VET systems with staunch employer engagement, while others have not. But with variations between countries where one would expect consistency based on similar governance and economic systems—and vice versa—there are no easy explanations. The best I can offer is a broad proposition that countries must have the right combination of social norms, legislative regulation, formal incentives, and broad cultural beliefs about the purposes and goals of education. The reasons certainly are not based in history, as all countries had apprenticeships prior to the development of universal public upper secondary schooling. Indeed, all still have some forms of apprenticeship for the trades, which may now be carried out by labor unions alone or are integrated with high school or upper secondary education. There is simply no comprehensive explanatory theory.

According to Stefan Wolter and Paul Ryan, two of the leading economists studying these issues, such a theory would have to take into account the following factors:[12]

- Labor market regulation (no external training standards versus enforced external standards)
- The skill requirements of production, given technology and job design
- Substitutability in production between trainee and other labor (skilled and unskilled)
- Asymmetric information about the content of training programs
- Alternatives open to trainees (full-time education and unskilled employment)
- Monopsony power of firms over trainees, not just over skilled workers[13]

But no such analysis now exists. Despite the lack of a detailed theory, the first factor on Wolter and Ryan's list—labor market regulation— is a frequently cited barrier to engaging employers among countries interested in building more comprehensive apprenticeship systems. Whether, and to what extent, the government regulates wages, union- ization, and industry's ability to hire and fire are all culprits.

Economists studying German and Swiss VET systems have done the most extensive studies on the economics of apprenticeship—particu- larly on what motivates firms to take on apprentices. A major variable in all such studies is the degree to which the decision to train young people is linked to the costs of labor market regulation, and how that influences policy.[14] In countries with strong worker protections, the costs of dismissing an employee are high, unions have considerable power against group dismissals, temporary employment is restricted, and there is low worker mobility. Under these constraints, employers benefit significantly from getting to know potential employees as ap- prentices before deciding whether to hire them as regular employees. There is no obligation to keep apprentices on beyond the training period. When firms do hire former apprentices, turnover declines be- cause former apprentices stay longer in their training firms than new hires, and companies have a better match between the employee's skills and the firm's needs.

In lightly regulated countries, companies reap other benefits or they would not train at all, since they are free to hire and fire as they wish and do not pay so much for hiring errors. As an indicator of regulatory differences, the OECD provides country rankings for the strictness of labor market protection legislation, based on three characteristics. (See figure 2.1.) The United States ranks first, with the least regula- tion, while Australia and Switzerland are sixth and seventh, and the Netherlands, Germany, and Norway are seventeenth, nineteenth, and twenty-first of the twenty-eight OECD countries listed.[15]

In "Going Separate Ways? School-to-Work Transitions in the United States and Europe," two OECD economists note that in coun- tries with highly regulated labor markets and strong apprenticeship systems, large proportions of youth succeed in integrating into the job market relatively quickly, and youth unemployment is low. (About 90

FIGURE 2.1 The overall strictness of employment protection legislation and its three main components, 2003

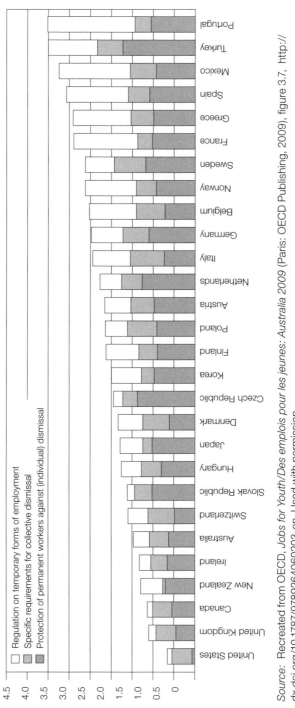

Source: Recreated from OECD, *Jobs for Youth/Des emplois pour les jeunes: Australia 2009* (Paris: OECD Publishing, 2009), figure 3.7, http://dx.doi.org/10.1787/9789264060203-en. Used with permission.

percent of young people ages fifteen to twenty-four were employed over a five-year period.)[16] In these highly regulated countries, apprenticeship is a key component of a youth policy that supports young people's transition to the world of work and productive adulthood, while also respecting culture and laws that seek to protect adult employees from the capriciousness of the market.

The OECD researchers go on to contrast these strong VET countries with countries that have highly regulated labor markets but *do not have* strong work-based training as part of the formal school system. In Italy, France, and Spain, where apprenticeships are rare, they note, between 25 percent and 40 percent of young people are unemployed or inactive.

In these countries, employment contracts of "indeterminate duration," which actually equate to lifetime tenure in a job, are the norm. The policy recourse such countries use to address youth unemployment is to implement highly regulated temporary contracts: under special circumstances, employers can hire young and inexperienced people for short-term employment. Consequently, young people may enter a dual labor market with a sector of permanent and well-protected jobs divided from a secondary sector of temporary and less secure employment. They may be employed in various short-term jobs over a period of several years.

In France, even highly educated young people queue up for jobs, sometimes waiting years for a position to open due to a retirement. David Bell and David Blanchflower's recent research on labor market institutions and youth unemployment shows that employment protections, legislation, benefit replacement rates, and tax wedges in eighteen OECD countries, including the United States, do not explain unemployment rates, although they do influence the shape of various pathways to jobs.[17] This conclusion indirectly supports apprenticeship as the decisive factor in hedging against youth unemployment.

It is easy to see why firms in highly regulated economies would benefit from training young people. Less intuitive—and important for U.S. policy makers to understand—is why companies would train in low-regulation countries. In a study of the financing of apprenticeship training in the light of labor market regulation, based on two identical firm-level surveys from Switzerland and Germany, the authors observe the following differences in motivation to train: "German firms are willing to finance apprenticeship training, whereas Swiss firms on average only train if the financial investment is offset by the productive contribution of apprentices" during training. That is, in highly regulated Germany, firms actually lose money on the training itself, but they recoup it in "post-training benefits," such as lower hiring and firing costs. In Switzerland, by contrast, where there is significantly less regulation, the apprenticeships must pay for themselves; apprentices must carry out work that adds to the firm's bottom line during their three-year training period.[18]

Figure 2.2 shows the increasing productivity of Swiss apprentices in programs of two through four years in length. The return to the firm increases with the growth of the apprentice's skills. By the end of the training period, apprentices are carrying out work that is highly skilled—at a wage that is substantially below that of a skilled regular employee—reaching about 75 percent of full productivity during the fourth year of an apprenticeship.

Additional comparisons between Germany, where labor market regulations make it difficult to fire people, and Switzerland, which is

FIGURE 2.2 Relative productivity of apprentices

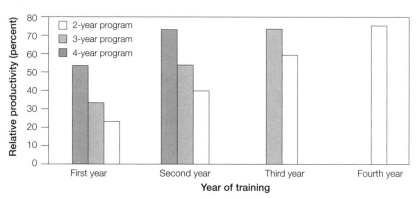

Source: Samuel Mühlemann, *Lehrlingsausbildung—ökonomisch betrachtet: Ergebnisse der zweiten Kosten-Nutzen-Studie* (Zürich: Rüegger, 2007). Used with permission.

more like the United States with few job protections, confirm the conclusions of *Jobs for Youth*, the OECD's sixteen-country series on transitions from school to employment. These countries produce similar successes in transitioning young people into work: both have the majority of young people in apprenticeships, and both have done well by their young people in a worldwide financial crisis that has produced the highest levels of youth unemployment ever recorded. In May 2010, Spain had an unemployment rate of 40.5 percent for people under twenty-five. Britain's was 19.7 percent in March, Germany's was 9.4 percent, and Switzerland's was 4.5 percent.[19]

INCENTIVES

While it is difficult to explain why some countries commit to workplace learning systems and others do not, it is easier to explain the motivations of individual companies. Research shows what incentives prompt those employers that train to do so—since the majority of firms do not. Below I discuss the use of various government incentive schemes and policies—including "training" wages—that incentivize some employers to train, and how employers offset the costs of VET.

Training Wages Minimize Costs to Companies

Whether a country has high, low, or modest labor market regulation, one way that VET systems control costs to employers is by permitting them to pay training wages acceptable to their unions. Training wages are generally lower than national average hourly wages, and available only to employees who are students in programs integrating learning and work. Generally negotiated between unions, employers, and the government, apprentice wages are set to be sufficient to attract good apprentices, but also to be reasonable to employers. Since apprenticeship wages usually rise during the apprenticeship period, how steeply they should increase is an additional policy decision.[20] For example, in Australia, the 2006 weekly rate for apprentices in their first year ranged from 47 percent to 75 percent of the national minimum wage, depending on the industry sector; by their fourth year, all apprentices receive the national minimum wage, or more.[21] In Norway, apprentices receive a wage negotiated in collective agreements between employers, unions, and the government. These range from 30 percent to 80 percent of the wage of a worker holding the qualifications sought by the young person, with the percentage increasing over the apprenticeship period.[22]

It is important to remember that apprentices generally live at home and are no older than nineteen or twenty. So while training wages are relatively low, they are still of high value to a sixteen-year-old and can go fairly far for someone of that age. By the time a young person is nineteen or twenty, their wages will have risen to near entry level.

The ubiquitous use of training wages for workplace learning over the years distinguishes the VET systems under study here from CTE provision in the United States. The inability of U.S. employers to pay lower-than-minimum wages to student trainees is a significant barrier to the country's development of a more comprehensive apprenticeship and workplace learning system that is part of a young person's schooling. The point here is not to pay low wages to young people who are entering full-time jobs, but to set apart under different regulations students whose work is required for completing a degree—in other words, *young people who are learning to work*. According to raisemywage.org, forty-five countries have training wages, usually with a mix of employment and age criteria.[23] The United States' policy and debate about it is briefly summarized in the box "Training Wages Could Boost U.S. Workplace Learning."

Many countries likely would justify the lower wages as an aspect of a broader youth policy that singles out the generation coming of age as requiring and deserving of special protections and supports. It is good policy to tie the successful transition of youth into the labor market to their future economic prosperity and that of their countries. More narrowly, lower youth wages can be justified on the grounds that an employer should be compensated for a young person's less productive work and the time spent in training him or her; young people are *students who are learning to work*, a different category than an entry-level adult employee.

Companies have to provide at least minimal training to new workers even if they are not apprentices, so some cost is required whether training is part of schooling or not. Nonetheless, in forming public/

Training Wages Could Boost U.S. Workplace Learning

The United States allows the payment of training wages, or subminimum wages, in certain, narrow circumstances. But opposition from across the political spectrum, not only from organized labor, has prevented the idea from gaining traction.

U.S. opponents of lower-than-minimum pay for young trainees have argued that a youth wage would lead to age discrimination, because employers would hire less costly teenagers in place of experienced adults, who need jobs to support their families. Going back more than thirty years, in response to a proposed amendment for a 75 percent minimum wage for workers under twenty years old, the New York Times argued, "A 40-year-old textile worker with a family has just as much right to a job as a 17-year-old high school dropout. There is no justification for Congress to give employers incentives to hire the young at the expense of others."[a] The underlying issue is, of course, job protection for adults. Despite little evidence either way, other opponents have argued that youth workers are just as productive as older workers, and so deserve full wages.

As a result of such arguments, the United States does permit subminimum wages, but the federal laws are extremely restrictive. Under the Fair Labor Standards Act, employers may pay employees under twenty years of age a lower wage ($4.25 an hour) for a limited period—ninety calendar days—as long as they do not displace other workers. The employer is not required to provide any training in this period.

As for student learners and apprentices, there are similar provisions. Students must be receiving instruction in an accredited vocational program affiliated with a school, college, or university, and can be employed on a part-time basis. The maximum amount of work time allowed is 240 hours, and the pay rate can be no less than 95 percent of the minimum wage. In

private partnerships with the state to take on apprentices, companies are committing to something quite different and more demanding than minimal training to get a young person the specific job–related skills needed for the moment. The investment is rather in breadth of education and training, and the goal is generally training for mastery, not just for immediately required skills.

Allowing a training wage is only one component of the policy set that makes up the package of incentives and supports for funding VET.

addition, the lower rate for a younger worker is an option only if an experienced worker is not available for employment. In any of these cases, employers must obtain a certificate from the U.S. Department of Labor for each student or apprentice employed at subminimum wages.

States make their own laws under the Fair Labor Standards Act, so there remains variation across the country. Oregon, for example, recently rejected any change to its law disallowing subminimum wages at all for youth. Michigan and Arkansas issue tax credits to employers of youth apprentices who are in a high school or GED program, perhaps to avoid the arguments made against subminimum wages.[b]

It is important to note, however, that U.S. employers do spend a considerable amount on training—but not for entry-level workers, and not often as part of degree or certificate programs. The American Society for Training and Development's (ASTD) 2010 *State of the Industry* report notes that "although organizations grappled with some of the worst economic conditions in several decades, business leaders continued to dedicate substantial resources to employee learning in 2009." According to ASTD, "U.S. organizations spent $125.88 billion on employee learning and development in 2009." This averages to about $1,081 per employee.[c] Training is targeted to ensure that middle- to high-level employees become more productive.

[a]"Minimum Wages for Youth, Students, and Trainees," The Minimum Wage: Information, Opinion, Research, http://www.raiseminwage.org/id37.html.
[b]Robert I. Lerman, *Training Tomorrow's Workforce: Community College and Apprenticeship as Collaborative Routes to Rewarding Careers* (Washington, DC: Center for American Progress, 2009), 27.
[c]Laleh Patel, "Continued Dedication to Workplace Learning," 2010 *State of the Industry* Report, *T+D*, November 2010, American Society for Training and Development, http://www.astd.org/TD/Archives/2010/Nov/Free/1110_2010+State+of+the+Industry.htm.

Other financial incentives have been put in place to offset the costs of providing on-the-job training. Beyond the cost of training wages, the full costs of VET are difficult to disentangle either per company, per student, or comparatively across countries. But some generalizations are possible. In most systems, the total costs of educating a VET student who has a substantial work placement are high—higher than a school-based program. Large and medium-size enterprises tend to spend more on training than small firms; training expenses are also skewed by industry sector. Training on heavy equipment or using scientific materials is expensive, as is training in some health professions that require intensive supervision as students learn to work with patients and clients.

The return to firms comes in student productivity, but that varies also. Training costs should diminish as the apprentice gains skills and becomes more productive: the first year will usually entail costs in a training organization, substantial time from a supervisor, and a low level of productive work, as well as expenses for mistakes. But by the third year (or fourth for some challenging and sophisticated fields), the apprentice likely will need little supervision and should be producing a substantial return. If policy permits the apprentice's wages to remain low, the gain to the company can be substantial. Many countries raise apprentices' wages closer to full entry level as their productivity grows over the years, so the gains to the company will be more in the intangibles—getting to know a potential employee, saving on hiring, and others discussed above.[24]

In some cases—as my interview journal shows—such as in highly competitive apprenticeship areas like graphic design, an apprentice may come to a company already highly skilled, but wanting the competitive advantage of entering the job market with an employer reference and work at a prestigious firm on her résumé. This was the situation of the young woman I interviewed at the 07 Group in Oslo. She had completed academic upper secondary school, had earned a university BA degree, and had taken an apprentice role to get work experience. Very soon after starting her apprenticeship at the 07 Group, she was assigned a client's project—to her delight and surprise—just as any more experienced designer would receive. Such apprentices add to the bottom line immediately and may compensate for young people needing substantial training.

Learning for Jobs enumerates the cost categories for training apprentices but notes that costs, just like benefits, are difficult to quantify beyond training wages. Among costs are the time of training supervisors and other employees who must provide instruction and explanation, teaching materials, administration of the program (usually a function of the human resources department in a larger company), and paying for mistakes in equipment breakdowns and wasted resources. Among other factors, these cost estimates do not take into account government spending on the infrastructure of VET, such as research, development of new competencies and assessments, and other costs, which are often shared between public and private entities.

Policy Trade-offs

Learning for Jobs provides a nice summary of the way countries make policy trade-offs:

> The quality of training needs to be sufficiently high to deliver benefits for the student and the economy, but not so high as to become an obstacle to employer engagement. Apprentice wages have to be sufficient to attract good apprentices and inhibit dropout, but not so high as to become yet another obstacle to employer provision. The apprenticeship period and its relationship to apprentice wages—which typically rise as apprentice skills develop—also need to be balanced. The apprenticeship period needs to be short enough to inhibit dropout into jobs by near-fully- trained apprentices, but not so short that the employer loses the productivity benefit of apprentices, which are largely obtained towards the end of the apprenticeship period, through the contributions of the trained apprentices.
>
> For employers, the net benefits of workplace training must yield sufficient incentive to encourage the provision of training places, but this can be achieved in different ways. For example this might involve (as in Switzerland) relatively low apprentice wages, balanced by strong requirements for training companies to prepare apprentice supervisors and adhere to the national curriculum. In Switzerland, this mix is deployed to support an apprenticeship system without recourse to subsidy. In Ireland, the government pays apprentices a stipend during their off-the-job training phases, making apprenticeship an attractive option in principle to both students and employers. (However, this position has been substantially challenged by the recent downturn in the Irish construction industry.)[25]

Table 2.1 compares the public cost of apprenticeship program completion per student in countries for which data is available.

TABLE 2.1   Estimated public expenditure on apprenticeship

In USD at purchasing power parity for GDP (reference year in brackets)

	1	2	3	4
	Average total cost of the program, per participant	*Cost of one year off-the-job apprenticeship, based on full-time equivalents*	*Program duration (in years)*	*On-the-job training (% of the program)*
Austria (2006)	15,300–15,900	n.a.	2–4 (depending on the program)	80%
Denmark (2008)	19,400–29,000	12,100	3.5–4 (typical duration)	40–60%
Ireland (2008)	19,000	16,300 (phases 4 and 6)	4 (typical duration)	70%
Netherlands (2006)	7,100–14,100	7,800	2–4 (depending on the program)	60%
Norway (2006)	36,200	12,900	4	50%
Switzerland (2007)	11,600–23,600	14,300	2–4 (depending on the program)	70%

Note: These costs include the cost of off-the-job education and training, provided in VET institutions. In countries such as Denmark and Switzerland this will represent the main public cost. In other countries, as in Norway and Austria, government also grants a subsidy to employers providing training to students and this cost is included in the figures. In Switzerland and the Netherlands training companies can benefit from a tax deduction, but the cost of these indirect financial incentives is excluded from the figures, as they are difficult to estimate; total costs for Switzerland and the Netherlands may therefore be underestimated. In Ireland, public expenditure covers education and training in VET institutions (instructor salaries, premises, equipment) and the allowances paid to apprentices.

Source: Recreated from OECD, *Learning for Jobs: OECD Reviews of Vocational Education and Training* (Paris: OECD Publishing, 2010), table 5.5, http://dx.doi.org/10.1787/9789264087460-en. Used with permission.

Other Financial Incentives

From a policy perspective, there are a variety of levers governments use to incentivize employers to engage: direct subsidies, tax breaks, training levies, and in-kind supports. Direct subsidies are set at a per-student rate and can offset training wages. Training levies are a redistribution mechanism—a tax on nontraining companies to support training. Sometimes levies are targeted to specific sectors to ensure the training of their own needed supplies of workers. In most strong VET countries, intermediary organizations also receive both company support and government funding to act as go-betweens, taking on some training, executing contracts, developing curriculum, and the like. These costs are difficult to estimate.

Finally, countries with strong youth policies may use a variety of strategies to promote equity by incentivizing companies to take students from vulnerable populations or underresourced regions. They also may put more money into the system during an economic downturn, when apprenticeship slots otherwise may dry up. Table 2.2 provides a snapshot of the combinations of policies used by a number of countries.

TABLE 2.2 How governments and employers support workplace training

	Public funding		Firms' collective contribution (e.g., training levy)	Employers' contribution to VET		
	Direct subsidy*	Tax deduction*		Training equipment	Salaries of trainers	Trainee travel expenses
Australia	Yes	Yes	No	Yes	Yes	Yes
Austria	Yes	Yes	In some sectors	Yes	Yes	Yes
Belgium (Fl)	Yes	Yes	No	Yes	Yes	Yes
Denmark	No	No	Yes	Yes	Yes	No
Finland	Yes	No	No	—	—	—
France	No	Yes	Yes	Yes	Yes	No
Hungary	Yes	No	Yes	Yes	Yes	Yes
Norway	Yes	No	No	Yes	Yes	Yes
Netherlands	No	Yes	In some sectors	Yes	Yes	Yes
Switzerland	No	Yes	In some sectors	Yes	Yes	Yes

Source: Recreated from OECD, *Learning for Jobs: OECD Reviews of Vocational Education and Training* (Paris: OECD Publishing, 2010), table 5.4, http://dx.doi.org/10.1787/9789264087460-en. Used with permission.

CONCLUSION

It would be fair to say that this chapter could be discouraging to U.S. readers interested in engaging employers in educating young people for work.[26] But it shouldn't be. Rather, it should be a call to arms to educators and to the employers who complain about the skills of the youth they hire, but who have been largely absent from serving to train and educate them. The Georgetown Center on Education and the Workforce calculates that employers already spend over $400 billion a year in providing both formal and informal training to employees. But these are typically people who have already completed their schooling and are now working full-time. It should not be so difficult for employers to dedicate some of this investment to preparing young people without having to implement a full apprenticeship system.

The Georgetown Center projects that nearly half of the new job openings generated between now and 2018—14 million—will go to people with an associate's degree or an occupational certificate. Some of these "middle-skill" jobs actually pay more than jobs held by those with a bachelor's degree. In fact, 27 percent of people with postsecondary licenses or certificates—credentials short of an AA degree—earn more than the average bachelor's degree recipient. Demand for middle-skilled professionals is growing in a number of fields. Health care, for example, needs registered nurses and health technologists—positions that typically require an associate's degree including some practical or clinical training—and is expected to grow by 1 million jobs by 2018. There will also be job openings in fields like construction, manufacturing, and natural resources, though many will simply replace retiring baby boomers. These fields will provide nearly 8 million job openings, 2.7 million of which will require a postsecondary credential. In addition, a wide variety of jobs require IT credentials at the certificate or associate's degree level.[27] Again, these are jobs for which company-based training could readily be combined with schooling.

Young people choosing the jobs just mentioned would benefit greatly if employers and their trade associations were to take a much more active role in collaborating with community colleges and even high schools to identify the knowledge and skills that people need to work in their industry. Beyond specifying qualifications, employers could quite easily modify their workplaces to become more student friendly. Training for these jobs calls out for clinical practice and real-time experience among experts doing their jobs. Many employers could provide structured part-time employment linked to the student's program of study for most of these particular jobs. For while many U.S. students must work, to save money for college or to help their families make ends meet, no one helps them relate their work to their programs of study. In short, it is high time for business leaders and educators to stop the refrain of "it can't happen here." They must look at modifications and adaptations to the practices among employers in strong VET countries that might benefit both their bottom lines and the prospects of young people in this country.

3

State-Directed VET Systems

Formal Public/Private Partnerships in Action

In order for businesses to take major responsibility with a nation's education system for training the next generation of workers, they must have substantial formal power to make decisions in partnership with public entities. VET countries structure their relationships with employers in various ways that are encoded in governance arrangements. These arrangements are symbolized in the cultural, legal, and practical roles businesses play in relation to the state and the school system in defining, maintaining, and revising the qualifications for the occupations young people can choose to study. In some countries, employers play a minimal role in establishing qualifications. In others, it is significant.

Wolf-Dietrich Greinert, a German researcher, defined three models into which one can fit most VET systems: "the liberal market economy model, the state-regulated bureaucratic model, and the dual-corporatist model." He distinguishes among these as follows:

> In type A, the economy takes priority from a cultural perspective. Training is regulated primarily by market forces. The functional needs of the company or the actual job are the leading didactic principle; in type B, politics take priority from a cultural perspective. Training is primarily regulated by bureaucratic control. The academic principle is the main didactic tenet; in type C, society takes priority from a cultural perspective. Training is primarily regulated

by dual control, i.e. a combination of market and bureaucracy. The vocational principle is the determining didactic orientation.[1]

Here for simplicity's sake, I call these the market model, the school-model (which is what Greinert means by "academic" and "didactic"), and the state-directed model. While these labels are not perfect, they are useful in defining distinctive elements.

More specifically, in the market model, vocational training is company based and takes place with limited collaboration with the state. Links to the school system, to school diplomas, or to the curriculum are weak or nonexistent. Companies provide training as they wish to young people, and unions offer apprenticeships—usually in the traditional trades. In the market model, young people tend to be trained for the applied skills needed for a specific company's job so that the investment in specific young people remains within the company. Employers, rather than the state, regulate certifications or qualifications; thus the match between skills and training is left to the market. England's system is an example of this model.

In the school model, the state provides initial VET through the school system, with light-touch internships, job shadowing, and both general- and career-focused course work leading to vocational preparation. Such a model characterizes the United States, France, Hungary, Korea, and Sweden. Students may learn for jobs, but employers are not engaged in any depth and have no authority over key aspects of preparation—from curriculum to assessments to quality. They are the prospective "consumers" of prepared students.

Most complex—and with the best results—is the state-directed (but not state-run) model because it involves public and private entities working in partnership with checks and balances that ensure that the interests of all stakeholders are taken into account. This is the model for the strong apprenticeship or dual-system countries, as well as the model for countries with extensive school-based VET linked closely to labor market needs. This chapter explores the structure and roles of the major entities that make up the critical public/private partnerships that characterize state-directed VET systems—government, schools, employers, unions, and intermediaries.

More precisely, the chapter first describes the legal framework for state-directed VET systems and then turns to intermediaries, with a focus on their capacity, as important enabling and support organizations, to ease the burden on employers. These organizations present at the local or regional level have received little attention in accounts of the strong workplace learning systems; learning about their functions should help to answer some questions about how and why employers are willing to engage. Finally, the chapter offers some minicases from a variety of state-directed systems: the classic Swiss and German dual system, including an example of how Swiss employers engage in shaping training for entire professions; the Australian flexible "user choice" system; the Norwegian "two-plus-two" system; and the Netherlands' majority school-based system. (Readers will see that *state directed* does not mean *state run*.) I also include a section on costs of VET and incentives that lead companies to train.

While the systems profiled differ in the choices they provide young people, in each case the link to the labor market and the match between training and needed skills is ensured—as best as any training can be—by the public/private collaboration: the lead role played by private employers, with the state as the vigilant public partner, and the support of variously structured intermediary organizations.

THE STRUCTURE OF VET SYSTEMS

State-Directed Models

In general, in the state-directed model, the state establishes the legal framework for VET through a Vocational Training Act, setting up a tripartite governance structure: (1) the representative bodies established by the social partners (employers and unions), (2) the state (ministries, education boards at national and regional levels), and (3) VET providers (schools, state or regional entities). A study of five European countries (Austria, Denmark, Germany, Ireland, and the United Kingdom) identified the existence of a strong institutional and legal framework for apprenticeships as an important condition for the successful implementation of apprenticeship training: it sets out the roles of all stakeholders, the qualifications for teachers and trainers, the way VET is assessed, and how quality is controlled.[2] Such a legal document leaves little ambiguity about decision making and power sharing in specific realms.

Within the legal framework, the foundational document is the apprenticeship or traineeship contract that sets out the rights and obligations of both trainees and the firms receiving them. Table 3.1 presents some of the contractual characteristics of different workplace training arrangements. In general, students are responsible for finding a company that will provide them with workplace training, but they do

TABLE 3.1 Contracts for workplace training

Estimated percentage of VET upper secondary programs in workplace training by contract characteristics

	Mandatory	Non mandatory	Varies	Employer	Trainee	VET instruction	Employment	Training	Combining training and employment
Australia	■■	■■■		■■■■	■■■■	■■	—	—	■■
Austria	■■■■	■		■■■■	■■■■	■■■	■■	■■■■	■
Belgium (Fl)	■■		■■■	■■■	■■■	■■■	■	■■	—
Denmark	■■■■	—		■■■■	■■■■	■■■	—	—	■■■■
Finland	■	■■■■		■■■■	■	■■■■	—	■■■■	■
France	■■	—		■■	■■	—	—	—	■■
Germany	■■■	—		■■■	■■■	—	—	■■■	—
Hungary	—	■■		■■	■■	■■	—	—	■■
Netherlands	■■■■	—		■■■■	■■■■	■■■	—	■■■■	■■■■
Norway[1]	■■■■	—		■■■■	■■■	—	—	—	■■■■
Switzerland	■■■■	—		■■■■	■■■	—	—	—	■■■■

Note: Estimated percentage of VET secondary programs: — 0%; ■ 1–25%; ■■ 26–50%; ■■■ 51–75%; ■■■■ 76–100%.

1. Local government is also part of the contract.

Source: Recreated from OECD 2010, *Learning for Jobs: OECD Reviews of Vocational Education and Training* (Paris: OECD Publishing, 2010), table 5.3, http://dx.doi.org/10.1787/9789264087460-en. Used with permission.

receive help from their schools, guidance centers, or intermediary organizations that serve as brokers of apprenticeship places. The contract is signed between the employer, the apprentice, and sometimes also a legal guardian. Often the broker organization has the responsibility for ensuring that formal regulations are observed, and that standard procedures exist across firms in similar sectors—especially in regard to safety and quality of training of young people.

Figure 3.1 provides examples of the terms of apprenticeship contracts in three countries—Australia, Belgium (Flanders), and Austria.

FIGURE 3.1   Contracts for workplace training

In **Australia**, the Apprenticeship/Traineeship Training Contract is concluded between the employer and apprentice. A representative of the Australian Apprenticeships Centre advises both parties on their rights and responsibilities and ensures that the apprenticeship is appropriate to both parties. The contract outlines the employer's obligation to employ and train the apprentice, pay wages and ensure that the apprentice receives adequate facilities and supervision. Employers must submit a training plan, endorsed by the concerned training provider (VET institution). The contract stipulates a probation period, during which either party can terminate the agreement.

In **Belgium-Flanders**, an apprenticeship contract is signed between the employer, the apprentice and for apprentices under 18, their parent or guardian. It must be concluded through an "apprenticeship counsellor" to be recognised. Apprentices receive an apprentice allowance from their employer (the amount depends on age and year of training).

In **Austria**, a training contract is between the employer, the student and their legal guardian. The apprentice receives health, accident, pension and unemployment insurance. The training relationship is regulated by the labour and social law, as well as particular employee protection regulations for young people. Apprentices are entitled to a salary determined through collective negotiation, which varies among occupations.

Sources: Department of Education, Employment and Workplace Relations (DEEWR) (2010), www.training.com.au; Flemish Ministry of Education and Training, Background report, *Learning for Jobs: The OECD Policy Review of Vocational Education and Training*, 2009, unpublished. Austrian Federal Ministry for Education, Arts and Culture (2010) Austrian Federal Ministry for Education, www.bmukk.gv.at/schulen/bw/bbs/ berufsschulen.xml#toc3-id4.

Adapted from OECD, *Learning for Jobs: OECD Reviews of Vocational Education and Training* (Paris: OECD Publishing, 2010), box 5.3, http://dx.doi. org/10.1787/9789264087460-en. Used with permission.

Among state-directed models, the state always has the guiding or oversight role, but the responsibility for actual practice is divided between in-school and company-based training. In-school learning generally falls to an education ministry that sets the general parameters, but in decentralized systems like those of Norway and Switzerland, responsibility devolves to the local or regional level while in France it rests with the central ministry. Company-based learning can fall to the labor and employment ministries, to education alone, as in both Denmark and Norway, or to a combined labor and education entity, as in the example of the Federal Office of Professional Education and Technology (OPET) in Switzerland, which is a branch of Economic Affairs. In some countries, additional ministries, such as agriculture and health, also play a role—for example, in the Netherlands, where there are special programs for VET students in agriculture.

Regardless of which ministries are responsible for VET, in every country, the workplace portion of VET is generally a matter for national, not local or regional, policy and oversight. Such centralization is necessary because standardized qualifications or competencies are required for various occupations, and these cannot differ by region, as noted in chapter 1. *Occupational requirements* are almost universally defined as the knowledge, skills, and competencies required for specific occupations, and lead to a state- and industry-recognized qualification. The state plays a regulatory role here and generally sets up the student assessment and quality assurance *system* working closely at the national level with organizations representing occupational or industry sectors or employers and unions, in general. These stakeholder bodies, called "social partners," have substantial advisory power and decision-making authority in some realms. The *content* of qualifications and the assessment of student outcomes always include representatives of businesses and unions working in partnership with educators. Figure 3.2 provides snap shots of the various kinds of organizations that partner at a high level with government.

INTERMEDIARY ORGANIZATIONS

In different ways, each of the strong VET countries has successfully created a role for employers and unions that makes the burden of

FIGURE 3.2   Examples of institutional frameworks for engaging employers and unions

Sectoral level:
The **Australian Industry Skills Councils (ISCs)** are privately registered companies run by industry-based boards of directors, mainly funded by the Australian Government. Eleven national ISCs cover the skills needs of most of Australian Industry. Their tasks include advising the government, Skills Australia (an independent advisory body to the government), and companies on workforce development and skills needs; supporting the development of training and workforce development products and services; providing training advice to enterprises; and working with different stakeholders to allocate training places.

In **Belgium-Flanders, sectoral agreements** are concluded between the government and individual economic sectors to establish a protocol of cooperation for two years. Topics covered include school-company collaboration and workplace training for apprentices, jobseekers, and employees. These agreements also shape the priorities of labor market policy. Sectors also operate sectoral funds with contributions from companies and employees, supporting, for example the training of current and potential employees, competence development in companies and school-company collaboration.

The **UK Sector Skills Councils (SSCs)** are employer-led bodies that set training strategies for particular sectors of the economy. Twenty-five licensed SSCs cover roughly 85% of the UK's workforce. SSCs are charged with determining the skills offer for their vocational area and have a lead role in determining the qualifications that deliver skills and are eligible for public funding.

Regional level:
Regional VET Centres in the Netherlands have representatives of (regional level) social partners in their supervisory board. Forty-six regional VET centers across the Netherlands supply all the vocational training schemes financed by the government at secondary level and provide adult education.

Source: Adapted from OECD, *Learning for Jobs: OECD Reviews of Vocational Education and Training* (Paris: OECD Publishing, 2010), box 6.1, http://dx.doi.org/10.1787/9789264087460-en. Used with permission.

educating young people worth the return. While the incentives to train differ from country to country, each country works to ensure that the number of apprentice or trainee places, as well as the career areas requested, meets labor market needs. Put another way, the slots available are a measure of activity in the economy, and countries can use this information to help young people choose an occupational area and to adjust the number of training slots. As described in the previous chapter, the basic vehicles ensuring sustained engagement include components that now should be familiar to the reader: an agreement by employers that good employees need broad academic skills and knowledge, whether embedded in workplace training or provided more traditionally at school; employer-developed and state-validated qualifications that define each occupation and serve the holder of the qualifications as currency in the labor market; a vocational education law spelling out respective roles of cooperating partners; and, described below, vehicles that ensure implementation—strong intermediary organizations and sustainable financing policies.

Intermediary organizations provide the "glue" between the state and the company, the public and the private entities. Intermediaries differ in form and specific responsibilities among countries, but all function to relieve some of the education and training burden that would otherwise fall on employers. The closest organizations the United States has to these are probably workforce investment boards and trade organizations. Both work as links between U.S. employers and employees, or they represent them—similar to the role of VET intermediaries. But in the United States, workforce investment boards exist largely to help low-income and hard-to-place workers, while trade organizations may accredit or license in various professions. Neither type of organization exists to support the education of a wide range of young people.

Among VET countries, a wide variety of intermediary organizations have evolved—called variously chambers of commerce, sectoral organizations, knowledge centers, professional organizations, or training organizations—differing in form and specific responsibilities. They are generally private, not-for-profit entities that partner with employers and government bodies. In some countries, intermediaries are organized by region and serve employers in multiple fields with responsibilities that go beyond apprenticeship training to include regional economic development, business planning, and marketing. Most are organized by economic sector—more in the vein of trade associations in the United States—and each provides expertise within a limited range of related occupations. Some countries have a variety of types involved.

Australia, for example, has a large number of sectoral, or industry-based, organizations—of two types: (1) registered training organizations (RTOs), which work on behalf of companies to market and provide comprehensive training that leads to the country's vocational qualifications; and (2) group training organizations (GTOs), which select and employ apprentices, whom they then hire out to companies, saving the companies administrative time and responsibility. Norway has training offices that perform similar functions. In Switzerland, groups of companies form training associations that facilitate the sharing of apprentices for companies too small to take on full-time students themselves. Switzerland provides a subsidy during the association's first three years of operation to incentivize firm participation. (Detailed information on intermediaries in specific countries follows this overview.)

The driving purpose of intermediaries is to ensure that apprentices and trainees attain the appropriate qualifications for each legally defined occupation, working with, and on behalf of, the member companies they represent. The qualifications represent the employers' statements of required learning outcomes and provide a road map for all training. Intermediaries usually have statutory authority for particular aspects of VET. As go-between organizations, they may do any or all of the following: find apprenticeship workplaces, provide orientation for young people starting apprenticeships, execute contracts between employers and apprentices, provide general training in the basics of a career area, develop curriculum, carry out assessments in partnership with educators, and represent their occupation or sector in the development and validation of qualifications.

Without such intermediary organizations, employers likely would be unable to provide education and training to young people and to keep the training up to date. The responsibility would be overwhelming, and achieving consistency across similar industries would be time-consuming and probably impossible. In other words, these intermediary organizations are critical to sustaining a VET system. Any country wishing to build a strong workplace learning sector will need to learn how these organizations function, how they are sustained, and what status they have as the go-betweens or linchpins of the systems they support. The country profiles below describe how VET is provided, with a special emphasis on the role of intermediaries, which is little known or understood by most U.S. readers and may help them to understand how employers can manage to train (especially small to medium-size enterprises) without having major human resource departments.

COUNTRY PROFILES—WHERE VET IS STRONGEST

Germany and Switzerland: The Classic Model

System Overview. Germany and Switzerland represent the classic apprenticeship model: a dual system where teens attend school one or two days per week, and learn in the workplace three or four days per week, over a period of two to four years. Participation rates are high. Nearly 60 percent of upper secondary students in Germany take part in VET and about two-thirds of upper secondary students enroll in Switzerland. In Germany, about 1.6 million student trainees are studying for about 360 different recognized training occupations. About 484,000 companies, or 23 percent of all companies, provide training.[3] In Switzerland, a much smaller country (7.6 million people, as opposed to 80 million in Germany), in 2010, about 226,000 students were training for 250 different occupations. About 30 percent of companies participate in the apprenticeship system.

One qualitative difference between the German and Swiss systems is the robust pathway developed in Switzerland over the last decade from VET to professional education and training (PET) in the nine universities of applied sciences (UAS). These institutions offer practical, university-level education, and are designed to serve employer needs, to carry out applied research, and to be engines of innovation for the economy. They raise the status of upper secondary VET in that they provide an attractive pathway from the vocational education system to a nationally recognized qualification at the tertiary level, leading to a specialization or a managerial position. To qualify, VET students must complete the three- to four-year Federal Vocational Baccalaureate, awarded to VET graduates with strong academic skills. About 50 percent of students who earn the Federal Baccalaureate enroll in a UAS either immediately after completing their apprenticeship or after several years of work experience.[4] There are about 400 PET programs in fields such as technology, economics, design, health, social work, and the arts, all leading to professional college degrees.

Such pathways are an aspiration in Germany, but have been much slower to develop there. Indeed, according to *Learning for Jobs, Germany,* in 2009, only 23 percent of a typical age cohort completed a tertiary education program compared to an OECD average of 39 percent. Among students without university entrance qualifications but with a VET diploma, only around 2 percent made their way into tertiary education.[5] *Learning for Jobs* argues that many more German VET graduates should be participating in tertiary education given the high standards of VET, and surmises that there may be artificial barriers to participation: lack of information, confusing heterogeneity across *Lander* (states) of kinds of institutions and programs, costs of tertiary education, and a perception that VET graduates' skills are too low.[6]

Vocational Training Acts

In Germany, as in Switzerland, a Vocational Training Act spells out detailed rules for establishing occupational titles, training content, and training duration, as well as examination or assessment standards stipulating the requirements to be met for certification. They also prescribe mechanisms, modalities, and procedures for examination. In both Germany and Switzerland, VET qualifications are highly portable within the country and, increasingly, abroad. Their portability depends on the engagement of employers and unions as central partners in designing, implementing, and monitoring training. In Switzerland, students successfully passing their VET exams gain the right to use the legally protected words *qualified professional* in whatever field they have chosen as a concentration. In Germany, an individual's *Beruf* or "calling" signifies "a body of systematically related theoretical knowledge (Wissen) and a set of practical skills (*Konnen*), as well as the social identity of the person who has acquired these. Achievement of such an identity is certified by a diploma upon passing an examination and is on this basis recognized legally and without question by all employers and goes together with a particular status and wage grade."[7]

Intermediary Organizations

In both countries, chambers of commerce or professional organizations play a major convening role for the state and other VET partners. Although they are private entities, these organizations function as public bodies in training matters. Thus, in both countries, they have statutory responsibility for developing the workplace curriculum; accrediting training companies; assessing, testing, and certifying the qualifications of students in partnership with the state; and maintaining training centers. However, they function somewhat differently in each country.

There are around eighty German Chambers of Industry and Commerce, and all businesses in Germany must belong to one. The umbrella organization, DIHK, speaks for 3 million businesspeople.[8] German chambers operate regionally, and VET is only one—albeit the most prominent—of their six responsibilities, along with regional economic development, business promotion, international relations, legal matters, and innovation. Companies pay a means-tested fee that supports their chamber's work. Beyond their basic VET functions, chambers may also serve as advisers to families and companies seeking apprenticeships, employ training consultants, and provide up-to-date labor market information for the sectors active in their regions. For example, they may mount seminars on new technologies or provide foreign-language courses. Assessing apprentices is a key function: German chambers maintain about 20,000 examination committees, which conduct 360,000 exams per year.[9]

In Switzerland, the professional organizations are structured around clusters of industries or occupations, rather than by region, and have a more focused educational function. Their sole role is to develop and maintain the VET system. In particular, they focus on defining and supporting apprenticeships, as well as working with students completing upper secondary diplomas. (See the box "Swiss Intermediaries: A Lead Role in Revamping Commercial Training for the Twenty-First Century.") The Swiss organizations also differ from German chambers in that they collaborate in order to set up traineeships at the BA level in partnership with the UAS.

Swiss Intermediaries: A Lead Role in Revamping Commercial Training for the Twenty-First Century

Representing employer and union interests, Swiss intermediaries, organized by occupational sector, have a formal convening role with the public and private entities when it comes to starting a new professional training program or revising one that is out of date. Support and guidance come from the Federal Office of Professional Education and Technology (OPET), a branch of the Federal Office of Economic Affairs. OPET is the federal government's arm for ensuring that "the Swiss VET/PET system produces qualified workers and that Switzerland remains an appealing and innovative location for both economic activities and education."[a] (Readers should note that unlike in the United States, vocational education and economic activity sit in the same government agency.)

The collaborative work required to develop or revise apprenticeship qualifications and training sheds light on how entities work together. The revision process begins when a sector organization makes a formal request to OPET to establish a commission for a VET ordinance, the legal document that contains the required components of the occupation. OPET handles about twenty-five new occupations or revisions each year, with some revisions lasting several years, as in the case of basic commercial training.[b]

In Switzerland, basic commercial training is a vocational pathway that prepares thirty thousand young people annually to enter the job market through apprenticeships—or combinations of school and work. Indeed, commercial training, including banking, retail, and public administration, is the most popular career choice of Swiss youth, comprising twenty-three different areas of specialization. In the late 1990s, through their sectoral organizations, Swiss employers requested that OPET put in place a process to revamp commercial training to meet the changing requirements of the evolving global market. They complained that teaching methods were too academic and that students were not being trained according to business's current professional needs. In a six-year process, representatives from each area of specialization came together with government and union officials to agree on a new occupational profile, required competencies, the core syllabus, a teacher-retraining plan, assessment standards, an examination process, and cost estimates for putting all of the changes in place in schools and workplaces.

All in all, around one hundred thousand people were involved in the piloting, rollout, and full implementation of the revisions: vocational trainers, apprentices, vocational teachers, school directors, cantonal representatives,

(continued)

employer and union representatives, and instructors for intercompany train-ing courses. Today commercial training includes the new goal of promoting autonomy and "business process thinking" among its sixteen- to nineteen-year-old apprentices; encouraging reflection and self-assessment in a re-quired "course journal"; putting learning into action from the start of the training; and promoting the use of the technical, social, and methodological skills acquired by learning to do independent work. The revision process also resulted in the formation of a Basic Commercial Training Syndicate, which includes unions and companies that did not belong to a specific sector within commercial training. A separate government-led examination board is responsible for assessing the results of training, and so checks and balances were structured into the process to ensure high quality.

There is more to the story of the reform of commercial training in Switzer-land. For example, if you go to the Web site of the Swiss Bankers Associa-tion and look under *training*, you will find a graphic illustrating all of the paths one can follow from the starting point of upper secondary basic banking training. The display highlights the many different banking, economics, and financial management pathways available—all the way through a doctor-ate—with an explanation of the choices and requirements of each. [c] In ad-dition, the site includes the entire modularized curriculum; the assessment methods and previous exams; responsibilities of both students and appren-tice trainers; and reference to the broader knowledge required to serve a bank well—an understanding of economics, law, and global change.

In their 2009–2010 Annual Report, the Bankers Association describes the Web site that is key to their student recruitment campaign. The site "sets out five good reasons for getting involved in basic bank training. This dynamic website, which is specially designed to appeal to young people, shows how exciting and diverse the three-year bank commercial training course . . . [is]. The site is informal and relaxed, with personal input from trainees, interns and training staff also giving a glimpse into the everyday ex-periences of young people during training."

[a]"Federal Office for Professional Education and Technology OPET," Federal Depart-ment of Economic Affairs, http://www.bbt.admin.ch/bbt/portraet/index.html?lang=en.
[b]Philipp Aggeler, project manager, Global and Bilateral Cooperation, OPET, "VET in Switzerland" (presentation for visit of Nancy Hoffman and Michael Maynard, Bern, September 30, 2010).
[c]"Education System in Banking Sector," SwissBanking, Swiss Bankers Associa-tion, http://www.swissbanking.org/en/home/bildungssystembank.htm; also see "Systemic Innovation in the Swiss Vocational and Professional Education and Train-ing System: Country Case Study Report," in *OECD/CERI Study of Systemic Innova-tion in Vocational Education and Training* (Paris: OECD Publishing, 2008), 18–23.

Beyond the Germanic Systems

The VET systems of Australia and Norway (whose profile follows) represent alternatives to the classic, well-known Germanic designs. Australia has a flexible user-choice system in which money follows the student, while Norway's two-plus-two model features a more standardized two years of schooling followed by two years of apprenticeship.

System Overview. Australia has a broad marketplace of vocational training options, including state-supported apprenticeships, as well as independent and privately funded programs. The well-developed postsecondary or "tertiary" VET training system is carried out largely by technical and further education institutions (called "TAFEs") and over four thousand registered training organizations (RTOs). The Australian National Training Authority defines RTOs as intermediaries that function as "training brokers and facilitators" and as the "frontline" of VET, serving to translate industry needs "into client focused training and assessment," which the organizations provide to their clients.[10]

Within national guidelines, the six states and three territories of Australia vary in how they carry out VET. This system may have some lessons for the United States. Key features of the system are strong industry leadership, national quality assurance (in the form of registration/accreditation of training providers), and national training qualifications developed by industry with competencies for each qualification. Competencies and qualifications cover around 80 percent of occupations in Australia. As noted previously, over half of Australia's employers reported having used the VET system in 2009; they had jobs requiring a VET qualification, employed an apprentice or trainee, or had staff that undertook other nationally recognized training.[11] Over 50 percent of students age 17 or older (post high school) participate in a VET activity. Each year, 60 percent of upper secondary students are enrolled in VET, with about 40 percent undertaking an apprenticeship as part of a senior secondary certificate. This high school–level program including a school-based apprenticeship or traineeship is known as VET in Schools.[12] Australia explains the apprenticeship system to employers as in the schema illustrated in figure 3.3.

FIGURE 3.3 The pathway to employing an Australian apprentice

What is an Australian Apprenticeship?

An Australian Apprenticeship:
- Combines training and paid employment
- May lead to a nationally recognized qualification
- Is "competency based"
- Can be offered in a wide range of industries
- Training may be delivered either "on" or "off" the job (or both)
- Can be a pathway from school to work

For further information, you will need to contact an Australian Apprenticeships Centre.

What are the benefits of skilling an Australian Apprentice?

Benefits:
- Staff will be trained to meet your business needs
- A range of financial incentives and assistance may apply
- You get to choose the training provider and how, when, and where training is delivered.
- Training achieves nationally recognized qualifications developed by industry
- Over 600 qualifications available to match your requirements

Click here to go to the Australian Apprenticeships Pathways Web site where you can identify an occupation and underpinning qualifications relevant to your business.

For further information, please contact an Australian Apprenticeships Centre.

What are the costs of taking on an Australian Apprentice?

Benefits:

For training wage information and award details and information about conditions of employment visit the Fair Work Australia Web site OR call 13 13 94.

Training fees may be levied by a Registered Training Organization.

To contact a Registered Training Organization click here, to go to the Australian Apprenticeships Pathways Web site where you can select a State or Territory search.

How do I go about finding an Australian Apprentice?

There are a number of ways to find an Australian Apprentice. You can choose to . . . .
- Contact your local Job Services Australia provider
- Recruit someone you know or who has been recommended to you
- Advertise the position in a local paper or on job sites
- Contact your local Group Training Organization about hosting an Australian Apprentice
- Call an Australian Apprenticeships Centre
- Advertise your position on the Indigenous Employment Service Web site.

What do I do after recruitment?

As soon as you have found a person to fill your position, you will need to get them "signed up" through an Australian Apprenticeships Centre.

An Australian Apprenticeships Centre will organize a time with you and the apprentice/trainee for a representative to come out and explain the Training Contract.

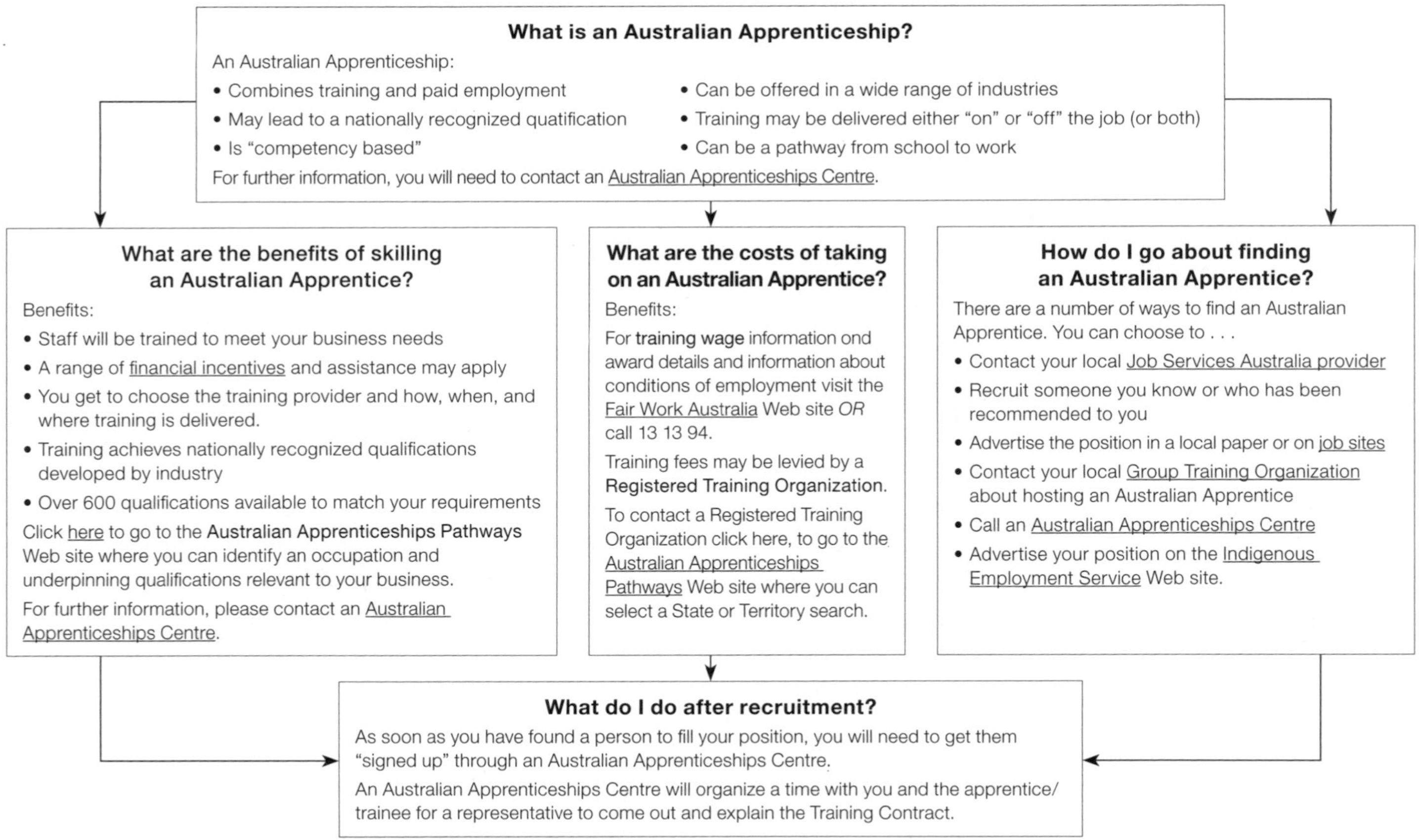

Source: Adapted from "Information for Employers Overview," Australian Apprenticeships, Australian Government, http://www.australianapprenticeships. gov.au/Info_Emps/Overview.asp#3.

Intermediaries. It may seem cleaner—and it is certainly less confusing—to have a single design for VET, as in Switzerland and Germany, where workplace learning is provided by a company and its intermediary organizations, and only a small number of students opt for school-based training alone. Australia has chosen to build a more versatile system, with multiple options for education and training. Under the principle of user choice, implemented nationally in 1998, employers and their apprentices/trainees together choose from an array of RTOs and group training organizations (GTOs), based on need, access, and compatible approach. The RTO is then responsible for the formal (usually off-the-job) training component and the work and learning arrangements in the company. Nonprofit, government-supported GTOs offer a different approach, employing apprentices themselves whom they hire out to companies for workplace experience, taking the burden of recruitment, contracts, and other human resource functions off the to-do list of employers. People of any age can be full- or part-time apprentices or trainees. Young people can combine part-time apprenticeship with the last years of high school or with technical postsecondary education, or they can enter apprenticeship after completing high school, with no further in-school training. The current government is encouraging further and faster growth of vocational education, building on the rapid growth in the last decade of the twentieth century when participation increased from one million enrolled to 1.7 million enrolled in 2002, or an increase of 62 percent.[13] In 2010, the latest year for which statistics are available, 1.8 million students were enrolled, an increase of 5.4 percent over 2009.[14]

In Australia, there is little distinction between training of young people and training of adults, or among the multitude of providers, since what matters are outcomes and qualifications obtained, not who provides the training or how they do it. As a report from Australia's National Center for Vocational Education Research (NCVER) notes, "VET can now no longer be defined as a distinct sector—many schools and most universities are or operate registered training organizations— many VET providers provide senior secondary schools programs and enroll large numbers of school-age students. Some VET providers are also accredited higher education providers."[15] Both for-profit and not-for-profit organizations can train, and businesses themselves have become RTOs in order to qualify to train their own employees, as in the case of Qantas described in chapter 1. Other variations among RTOs include organizations providing training for a specific industry (for example, health) or a specific learner group (such as police, emergency service personnel, disadvantaged learners, or indigenous Australians).

It is the responsibility of each registered training organization to teach and assess as it sees fit.[16] To become registered, an RTO must get government approval for the specific qualifications and units of competency that it wants to assess and certify. RTOs provide qualifications within the Australian Qualifications Framework and Statements of Attainment that are recognized and accepted by industry and other RTOs throughout Australia. (See the box "CIBs, VTOs and Qualification Documents" for an example from New South Wales.)

Such Statements of Attainment are the currency for an individual's entry into a chosen field in the labor market. A search of the Internet for Australian training packages in fields such as accounting, IT help desk, or nursing assistant reveals a wide array of choices, including an array of postsecondary options, a variety online. However delivered, each package has a code and title designating the name of the particular qualification, the competencies numbered to indicate where they fit in the qualifications scheme, and a level within the Qualifications Framework. (See an example of certification in clinical coding in figure 3.4.)

Australian employers and unions are engaged through a number of vehicles at the national, state, and local levels in the development of VET policies in partnership with the government. In general, as in other VET countries, employers and unions do not participate individually, but rather through various intermediaries in which the common interests of a sector are represented. They include such organizations as the Australian Chamber of Commerce and Industry (ACCI), with a member network of over 350,000 businesses; the Australian Industry Group (AiG), which represents about 10,000 employers in manufacturing, construction, automotive, telecommunications, and information technology, including call centers, transport, labor hire, and other industries; the Business Council, an association of the chief executive officers of 100 of Australia's leading corporations, with a combined

CIBs, VTOs, and Qualification Documents

Each state in Australia issues its own VET information within the national framework as in the example below from New South Wales:

Commissioners Information Bulletin (CIB)
A CIB contains information for the administration of apprenticeships and traineeships in New South Wales. The CIB specifies the training framework, industrial arrangements, job descriptions, licensing and regulatory requirements, resources to support the delivery of training, and training providers available to deliver the training.

Vocational Training Order (VTO)
A VTO is the legal instrument that establishes apprenticeships and traineeships in New South Wales. The VTO specifies the qualification, length of apprenticeship or traineeship, and probationary period.

Qualifications
Qualifications are formal certificates issued by a registered training organization when a person has successfully completed an educational program. Qualifications awarded to apprentices and trainees are industry-based, with specified combinations of units of competency required by each industry for each qualification. They are assessed by demonstrating competence of skills and knowledge under workplace conditions.

Source: Adapted from https://www.training.nsw.gov.au/cib_vto/index.html.
© State of NSW, Department of Education and Training.

workforce of over 1 million (about 10 percent of the labor force); and the National Farmers' Federation (NFF). In addition, Skills Australia, an independent statutory body, provides advice to the Minister for Tertiary Education, Skills, Jobs and Workplace Relations on Australia's current, emerging, and future workforce skills needs and workforce development needs.

Employers and unions are also members by statute of various national advisory bodies, including the eleven industry skills councils (ISCs), which provide industry intelligence to the VET sector about current and future training requirements, including industry skill reports. A specific responsibility of each industry skills council is development

FIGURE 3.4 Sample statement of attainment

Jane Smith

has attained

Clinical Coding Skill Set

HLTCC301A	Produce coded clinical data
HLTCC401A	Undertake complex clinical coding
HLTCC402A	Complete highly complex clinical coding

These units from the Health Training Package (HLT07) meet industry
requirements for clinical coding in the health industry

(Optional: These competencies form part of the
[insert code and title of qualification(s)])

(Where relevant: These competencies have been delivered
and assessed in [insert language].)

Dated 30 September 2007

Authorized Signatory Issuing Body

Nationally Recognised Training logo

State/Territory Training Authority logo (optional)

This Statement of Attainment is recognized within the
Australian Qualifications Framework

Source: Adapted from *Implementation Handbook*, 4th ed. (Carlton: Australian
Qualifications Framework Advisory Board, 2007), 80.

and maintenance of national training packages. This provides employers with a formal mechanism for identifying the competencies and qualifications they need and incorporating them into national training packages, promoting the critical alignment between what VET students learn and the skills and knowledge employers seek.

As in a number of countries worried about keeping young people in school and preparing them for jobs in the fiscal crisis, a VET reform process is under way. The call for change stems from criticism in the last decade that the training packages have become too complex, too skills specific, and too lengthy. The Australian National Quality Council (NQC), a committee of the Ministerial Council for Tertiary

Education and Employment, which is charged with overseeing quality and national consistency in the application of the Australian Quality Training Framework standards, is leading the process. This decision-making body with stakeholder representatives accredits and registers training organizations. After two years of research, the NQC has designed a streamlined model for training packages. As NQC publications state, the new model:

- *Is easier to use.* Simpler language, less repetition, and greater consistency will make training packages much more user friendly and accessible.

- *Provides greater focus on assessment, knowledge, and foundation skills.* Targeted sections of the training package will make it easier for RTOs to address these issues.

- *Has more support for RTOs.* Companion volumes will provide detailed advice on the use and implementation of a training package. They will include guides on RTO implementation, learning strategies, knowledge, and assessment strategies, and will be released concurrently with each training package.[17]

Norway

System Overview. Norway's two-plus-two system is structured with two years of school followed by two years of apprenticeship. An apprentice's first year is a learning year, while the second is as a full employee earning between 30 percent and 80 percent of the regular wage, negotiated collectively, with the percentage growing over the apprenticeship period. The two-year apprenticeship follows completion of a national curriculum tailored to each occupation. Upper secondary VET ends with a final examination that leads to a craftsman or journeyman certificate in the field of study. The examination is prepared and assessed by a trade-specific examination board appointed at the county level. Virtually all students who take the exam (96 percent) pass, and thus those who stay in the system come away with a recognized qualification. Legally, apprentices are employees of the enterprise, with conditions specified in a contract that is signed by the student, the company, and the county. (In Norway, each of eighteen counties has responsibility for upper secondary schooling in its region, both VET and gymnasium or academic high school.)

Intermediaries. Norway has a system of cooperative decision making, mandated by the Norwegian Education Acts, and of centralized negotiations involving both employers and unions on matters of education and training, as well as on wages and working conditions. With attention to student voice, the School Student Union of Norway (Elevorganisasjonen) is represented in both the National Council for VET and the County Vocational Training Boards. The Ministry of Education plays the role of secretary of the National Council for Vocational Education and Training. This agency comprises representatives of the nine vocational councils, one for each industry sector: building and construction; design, arts, and crafts; electricity and electronics; health and social care; media and communication; agriculture, fishing, and forestry; restaurant and food processing; service and transport; and technical and industrial production. The councils represent the formalized cooperation with the different stakeholders in Norwegian VET and provide advice on curriculum and qualifications in particular trades and occupations. Tripartite vocational training committees within each county have responsibility for implementing vocational training on behalf of the county authorities. Oslo is the only truly big city in Norway (population 580,000); many municipalities are remote—reachable by water or over mountainous roads, and employers are overwhelmingly small businesses.

To manage training, Norwegian industry councils establish training offices to serve groups of employers who could not take on a rigorous training curriculum alone because they are too small or not well equipped for such work. Training offices work actively to identify potential new training companies and establish new apprenticeship workplaces, supervise companies with apprentices, and train staff involved in the tutoring of apprentices. Like sectoral organizations in other countries, training offices in Norway often organize the theoretical part of the apprentices' training. They may also sign the apprenticeship contracts on behalf of smaller training enterprises, thereby becoming accountable for completion of the training and its results.[18]

Despite a structure that is clear and easy to understand, the Norway VET system has its challenges. The two years of school-based VET are often only loosely coupled with apprenticeships, with limited interaction between VET teachers and company-based trainers who take on students after their two years of schooling. In addition, instead of applying for an apprenticeship during their second year of VET, about one-third of students in VET choose a general supplementary course in the third year, switching to the pathway into tertiary education. Dropout rates from VET are higher than from the academic track. The Norwegians are concerned about the noncompletion rate from VET: further research is needed to ascertain whether students simply change their minds about what career they wish to pursue and go on to a university—an acceptable outcome—or simply leave school, perhaps because they don't get their first-choice apprenticeship.[19] If there is a lesson here for the United States, it is that students become more invested in apprenticeship systems that integrate work and learning from the start, and Norway is beginning to experiment with such a model in a new facility being built in Oslo.

The Netherlands

System Overview. The Netherlands has excellent results with the transition from school to work, with a system that provides choices between school-based and company-based VET, both with substantial workplace learning. The country has low youth unemployment and high postsecondary completion rates, despite a system with early tracking and multiple choices within tracks. At age twelve, based on a test, Dutch children are placed into one of three pathways: a scientific route to a university, higher general education, and intermediate prevocational education. Within the intermediate track (called VMBO), there are an additional four choices for twelve-year-olds: basic, supervisory, mixed, and theoretical vocational education. For students completing VMBO at age sixteen, there is still another set of vocational education choices, these lasting from six months to four years, again based on distinctions between assistant, basic, full professional, or middle management and specialist training, and on whether a student wishes to be in school with required workplace experience or in a firm as an apprentice with limited time spent in school. The

FIGURE 3.5 Overview of the Dutch educational system

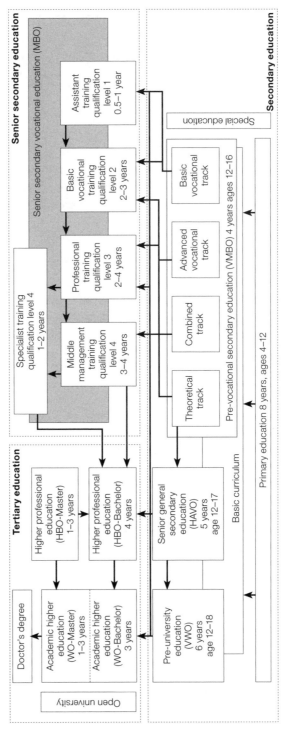

Source: Adapted from Colo, *Prepared for the Future* (Zoetermeer, Netherlands: Colo, 2008), http://www.colo.nl/publications.html. Used with permission.

longer VET programs lead to baccalaureate-granting higher-education institutions rather like the Swiss universities of applied sciences. Figure 3.5 illustrates the multiple pathways through the Dutch VET system.

Of the 480,000 Dutch VET students starting upper secondary school at age sixteen in 2007, nearly 70 percent were in vocational pathways with just over a third of these in apprenticeships (meaning that their learning is launched from the workplace rather than from school). However, both the school-based and the workplace routes require students to spend a substantial part of their time in work settings; the school-based pathway entails 20 percent to 60 percent of hours at a work site, for which the student receives a small stipend. In the apprentice pathway, students generally work four days per week, about 80 percent of their time, under contract to an employer who pays the minimum wage. Both groups obtain the same diploma.[20] Both the public and the private sector have put more money into senior secondary vocational education in recent years. The impulse of the private sector lay in making more money available for work placements. In addition, the government earmarked funding for projects such as improving various aspects of the transition from school to the labor market, and reducing the number of pupils dropping out of school.

Intermediaries. In the Netherlands, employers play a major role in VET. This is particularly relevant to the United States because the majority of young people choose a school-based option; schools must interact with employers to place students—a process that has been challenging in the United States. With this great variety of arrangements all requiring different kinds of workplace training, and without registered training organizations as in Australia, the Netherlands still manages a true delegation of responsibility for VET to employers. The key in the Netherlands, as in other countries with strong workplace learning systems, is a type of intermediary organization.

The Netherlands has seventeen sectoral organizations called Centers of Expertise on Vocational Education, Training and the Labor Market, which support employers in taking on student workers. The centers have a statutory responsibility to link education and the workplace and are responsible for developing the training requirements and qualifications for senior secondary vocational education. They provide the glue between industry and education. Under the umbrella organization known as "Colo," the centers jointly represent more than forty different branches of industry and constitute around 80 percent of economic activity in the Netherlands. The centers support over two hundred thousand accredited work placement firms in training five hundred thousand students at the senior secondary vocational level. Furthermore, Colo describes its mission as serving as a platform to discuss and agree on common interests, share best practices, and initiate new projects. Colo also serves as an accrediting body for work placements. The Netherlands' educational legislation stipulates that companies that train and supervise participants under the preparatory secondary vocational education (VMBO) and senior secondary vocational education (MBO) systems must obtain accreditation from a center of expertise, one of the organizations under the Colo umbrella. The accreditation is intended to certify that the company is a safe learning environment and that trainers agree to participate in a course before working with and supervising young people.[21] Figure 3.6 walks employers through a series of questions they should answer in anticipation of a decision to train.

Today's structure for VET in the Netherlands is the result of a 1996 reform that responded to a growing mismatch between education and the labor market. The WEB Act specifically required that "qualifications be portable, broad and flexible to cope with change and employability; and that business and industry have significant influence at all levels of the VET system."[22] But this employer role, like the roles described in other strong VET countries, is embedded within a broader social partnership in which employers and unions participate in decision making and take responsibility for the well-being of the youth of their country. The centers of expertise thus must work within a broader frame to prevent the qualifications under development from becoming too narrow and job or firm specific. (More detail on how the Netherlands pays for VET is included in the cost section below.)

The Costs of VET—and Incentives to Train—in Strong VET Models

The previous chapter noted briefly the ways that governments incentivize and support employers to take on training: direct subsidies, tax breaks, training levies. Some countries provide extensive supports in curriculum

FIGURE 3.6   Becoming a training company

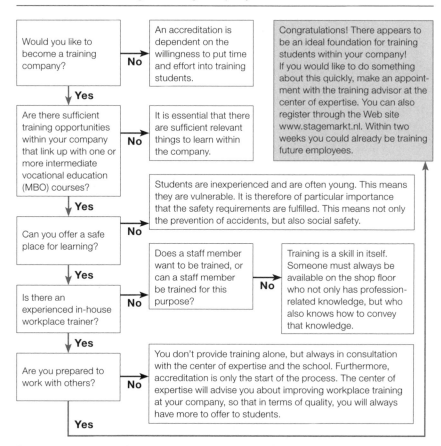

Source: Adapted from Colo, http://www.colo.nl/workplacement.html. Used with permission.

development, assessment, research, trainer education, and the like. Below, I describe the most frequently used of these policy levers in the strong VET countries.

Per-Student Subsidies: Norway

Per-student subsidies are a common way to use public funds to encourage companies to take on apprentices. In Norway, apprentices legally are employees of the enterprise, with conditions specified in a contract signed by the student, the company, and the county. Apprentices receive a wage negotiated in collective agreements that ranges from 30 percent to 80 percent of the wage of a regular worker, with the percentage increasing over the apprenticeship period. To help cover the costs, employers taking on apprentices receive direct subsidies from their county, which in turn receives a block grant for VET from the central government. The basic subsidy in 2008 was NOK 99 577 (ca. EUR 12,700) per apprentice/trainee. This covers the two years of the apprenticeship and is equivalent to the cost of one year in school. In addition to the basic subsidy, the training company receives up to NOK 41 568 (ca. EUR 5,300) per apprentice/trainee for training in specific crafts that the country wants to preserve. Governments can manipulate subsidies from public funds as the economy changes, such as doing more to incentivize employers to take apprentices during a downturn—as in the current fiscal crisis.

Multiple Strategies: The Netherlands, Australia, Austria
Some countries—the Netherlands, Australia, and Austria—use multiple incentivizing strategies to encourage employer participation. In the Netherlands, 68 percent of upper secondary students participate in VET, of which one-third are in workplace apprenticeships. The Netherlands provides both subsidies and tax deductions for VET companies—a more complex system than Norway's but one worth the scrutiny of U.S. states or regions interested in engaging employers in workplace training. The seventeen sectoral centers of expertise are subsidized by the government for specific functions and for per-student and per-company services—in other words, for the volume of work within their legal mandate. Centers are funded for the number of qualifications and competencies they develop and maintain, the number of employers they accredit, the number of apprentices they recruit for companies and successfully place, and for specific research and development activities. In addition, in some sectors, as part of the national negotiations with the centers, the government assesses a training levy of 0.2 percent to 0.5 percent for the specific center for special purposes, such as training the unemployed. In addition, companies offering apprenticeship training programs are eligible for a 2,500 euro tax deduction for each student they take on.

MBO is the most expensive form of further education: spending per student totaled nearly ten thousand euros in the last several years. According to Statistics Netherlands, in 2008 businesses spent 3.1 billion euros on education. Most of the funds, almost 2.1 billion euros, went to supervise students in MBO. Businesses also spent money on research they commissioned at universities. The government provided 544 million euros' worth of subsidies and tax cuts, which is 37 percent more than in 2007. In return for this support and to incentivize participation, training companies receive a tax break of 2,500 euros for each pupil participating in their program.[23]

In Australia, while about 40 percent of young people participate in an apprenticeship through school, the cost information should be interpreted with the caveat that most data does not differentiate between youth and adult participation. Indeed, the Australian government funds both initial VET (IVET) and continuing VET (for incumbent workers) as one line item in its budget. Australia also provides significant funding for continuing training rather than leaving that to employers.[24] In other words, VET is the country's comprehensive workforce development strategy available to Australians between the ages of fifteen and sixty-four. The federal government's office of Australian Apprenticeship provides a wide range of incentives for employers, largely in the form of subsidies. These include sums in the range of 1,200 to 1,500 Australian dollars for hiring, retaining, and graduating an apprentice. There are special subsidies for low-skilled candidates, for those with disabilities, and for companies hiring apprentices they have trained. RTOs also get bonuses for student completions, with incentives for more challenging students. In addition, RTOs and GTOs receive financial support from their states and the federal governments to assist with administrative overhead.[25]

In 2009, the latest year for which data is available, total recurrent expenditure on VET by Australian state and territory governments totaled $4.7 billion. Of this sum, $3.2 billion came from states and territories themselves and the balance from the federal government. Total government expenditure was equal to $317.57 per person aged fifteen to sixty-four across Australia. Of the approximately 1.7 million students who participated in VET, 1.3 million (about 75 percent) were government funded. The remaining 431,400 students participated on a fee-for-service basis as domestic students (22.5 percent of all VET students) or were international students (2.8 percent of all VET students).

Infrastructure Supports: Switzerland
Finally, some countries might be said to incentivize employers by providing extensive infrastructure supports rather than subsidies or tax credits. Switzerland is the best case in point, but Australia, Germany, and the Netherlands have research and development sectors devoted to VET. While Switzerland has apprenticeship wages at the low end and does not subsidize training places, the country appears to be without equal in government-funded "accessories" from which employers and students benefit greatly. The vignette portraying the reform of Swiss commercial training (see the box "Swiss Intermediaries: A Lead Role in Revamping Commercial Training for the Twenty-First Century" earlier in the chapter) demonstrates how the professional staff and organizational expertise of OPET managed the revision supported by the research of the "leading houses" (research institutes). OPET is also the engine of innovation in the VET/PET system; it has an agenda to revise legislation, increase the number of apprentice places available, and, more recently, promote Swiss VET internationally. Employers also benefit from the teacher-training, research, and support services of the Swiss Federal Institute for Vocational Education and Training.

In 2009, a total of CHF 3.4 billion (3.9 billion in U.S. dollars) was allocated to the VET/PET sector. (Some aggregate figures exclude PET; the investment then is roughly CHF 2.8 billion, or US$3.2 billion.) Under the new Vocational and Professional Education and Training Act (VPETA), the confederation's share of public funding for the VET/PET sector will be about one-fourth of the total cost. Ten percent of federal funding will be used to promote VET/PET development projects, as well as specific activities that serve the public interest.[26] There are difficulties in compiling figures for the private contribution. But according to one expert on the financing of Swiss VET, a rough estimate is that private and public spending are about equal (using the figure that excludes PET).[27]

Regulating Supply and Demand

In strong VET countries, a government entity keeps careful watch on the match between the supply of apprentices and demand for their services through regular public reporting mechanisms often called apprenticeship barometers. In Australia, Switzerland, and the Netherlands, among others, barometers report the number of apprenticeships open, changes in openings, and such data as completions by field, withdrawals, and qualifications received. The data can inform students, training developers, and providers, as well as warn a government that incentives for employer participation need adjustment. For example, in the Netherlands, Colo, the umbrella organization of the centers of expertise, reports four times a year on changes in the availability of apprenticeship placements and on-the-job training. More than eight hundred employees of the centers of expertise are involved in collecting labor market data, displayed by sector and region in the Colo barometer (see "Opportunities for Internships and Apprenticeships in the Netherlands by Sector" on the Colo Web site).[28]

With regular information coming in about demand and supply, countries can take steps to change their incentive structures as needed. Some adjustments are minor, resulting in a sectoral organization more aggressively soliciting its constituents to provide more work sites for a particular trade or occupation. Both Austria and Germany have experienced an oversupply of young people seeking apprenticeship placement in the last several years. In Austria, the Federal Ministry of Education, Arts and Culture appointed an experienced business leader to recommend policies that would incentivize employers to take on additional and harder-to-place apprentices. Today, Austrian employers who take additional apprentices receive monthly payments for them ranging between US$140 and US$570 a month. The government also provided more supports—apprenticeship advisers who solicit places for young people, pretraining to provide better-qualified students, and pathways into higher education. The reunification of Germany put pressure on the government to provide more places for students, and a queue for places developed, as a greater number of less qualified students sought apprenticeships. The German government addressed the problem by loosening some labor regulations and offering wage subsidies for harder-to-educate young people, a strategy many countries employ.

In economic crises, such as the one we are currently experiencing, countries may need to implement aggressive measures to ensure that young people have access to training places—that is, that they have youth policies and are committed to protecting young people in downturns, since this population group is hardest hit. (This book's final chapter, on youth left behind and at risk of failure in school and the labor market, describes a number of special measures countries take to provide workplace learning when slots become scarce.)

CONCLUSION

The partnerships that engage employers in the strong VET countries may appear to have few lessons for educators and business leaders in the United States. They may appear extremely complex and rooted in cultural and legal institutions that are alien to us. But it may be useful to suspend disbelief. In the systems profiled above, not just employers, but employer organizations including national umbrella organizations, regional training offices, and intermediaries serving occupational sectors or performing specific services to local training businesses play a major role. They represent their sectors in defining occupational qualifications, supporting and, in some cases, training apprentices, and providing workplace learning for school-based VET programs. While there is significant variation among the strong VET systems in the structure of employer "ownership" of the training system, in each case employers make a substantial contribution. The takeaway from this story, then, is that the benefits must outweigh the costs in order to make VET make sense, and they do.

The German Dual System

A U.S. Observer Reflects on a Strong VET System

By Robert B. Schwartz

In early February 2010, I spent a week looking at the German vocational education and training (VET) system. I was there as a member of the OECD team conducting a study of Germany for the OECD's *Learning for Jobs* review.[1] As the VET director in the state of Saxony told us at the beginning of an impressive daylong visit, one of the great strengths of the German system has been its policy stability and continuity.

My last look at the German VET system was twenty-five years earlier when I was part of a delegation of corporate and civic leaders from Boston that had come together to launch the Boston Compact. (The compact was an agreement struck between the city's employer community and its school system to provide preferred access to entry-level jobs in the downtown economy for graduates of the city's high schools in return for raising performance standards in the schools). What immediately struck me on this return visit was how many of the essential elements of the German system were still in place twenty-five years later. The dominant pathway for helping young people make their way from the completion of lower secondary school (typically, grade 10) into the adult workforce is still the *dual system*, in which young people combine work and schooling in a carefully crafted three-year apprenticeship program leading to a recognized qualification in one of 350 occupations.

Around 53 percent of young people today choose the dual system as their pathways through upper secondary education. Alongside the dual system there also exist full-time vocational schools, typically offering two- or three-year programs that focus primarily on preparing young people for health-care and commercial occupations. These schools serve another 15 percent of the upper secondary age cohort, meaning that two-thirds of all young Germans receive an occupational qualification by the time they are twenty. Only about a quarter of young Germans pursue a university education, a figure well below the average among OECD nations. Given the U.S. policy focus on "college for all" and the increasing pressure to ensure that all students leave high school "college ready," the German system hardly looks like a model worth studying. On closer examination, however, I would argue that, for all of the deep cultural and political differences in our systems, there is much we can learn from the Germans.

Let me begin by quickly acknowledging the two features of the German system that are understandably the most difficult for Americans to swallow. First, Germany still sorts its students into two or three different types of what we would call middle schools after grade 4. The academically strongest students are sorted into the *Gymnasium*, where, if successful, they will continue on through grade 12, obtain the *Abitur* diploma, and go on to a university. (Interestingly, 17 percent of *Abitur* holders enroll in the dual system upon graduation, obtain a vocational qualification, and then decide whether or not to pursue university studies). The middle group of students are assigned to the *Realschule*, where after five years (grade 10, age sixteen) they receive a certificate entitling them to pursue further education (possibly transferring to a *Gymnasium*, if their record warrants it) or vocational training. The weakest students are shunted off to the *Hauptschule*, where after grade 9 they receive a certificate entitling them to pursue vocational education. While this early sorting system is under attack from the left and shows signs of softening, with comprehensive schools serving all students beginning to appear in some regions and the *Realschule* and *Hauptschule* tracks being merged in others, the persistence of the *Hauptschule*, with its separate school-leaving certificate, is likely to remain a major barrier to achieving more equitable labor market outcomes, especially for children from immigrant families.

The second feature of the German system that is hardest for Americans to understand is the age at which young Germans are expected to choose an occupation. Most Americans instinctively recoil at the idea that a sixteen-year-old should be asked not only to choose an occupation, but to sign a contract with a specific employer, detailing the terms and conditions of the work and learning program he or she is expected to undertake for the next three years. While such contracts are not binding—roughly 20 percent of apprentices break their contract in the first year, most moving to other occupations they find more suitable—the pressure to choose not just a broad field in which to be trained but one of 360 specific occupations seems excessive.

So what can Americans learn from the German system? To answer this question, we must first translate the German (and European, generally) distinction between lower and upper secondary education into the American context. Lower secondary schools (the upper grades of the middle schools described above) end in grade 9 or 10. While it is generally recognized that students who complete an academic upper secondary education in Germany and obtain an *Abitur* are more comparable to students entering their sophomore year at an American university than to typical U.S. high school graduates, it may not be so obvious that upper secondary VET graduates have equivalent qualifications to U.S. young people with a vocational or technical degree or certificate from a community college. Indeed, at the high end of the apprenticeship continuum, like two students we met who were completing IT apprenticeships at Strato (Europe's second-largest Web-hosting company), apprentices leave the dual system with a set of technical skills and knowledge that would probably enable them to transfer into the upper division of a technical U.S. university. These students, both of whom had obtained the *Abitur* before beginning their apprenticeship, were in fact heading off to a university of applied science, the higher-education pathway for advanced careers in engineering and technology. While these two students were clearly exceptional, they are a useful reminder that the apprenticeship system serves the full range of occupations in Germany—white collar as well as blue collar, high tech as well as low tech.

The first thing to understand about the German system is that, although there is substantial variation across the sixteen states (*Lander*) and education is even more a state responsibility in Germany than in the United States, the VET system operates within a national regulatory framework, with responsibilities of the various parties clearly spelled out in law. Vocational schools, part-time or full-time, are the responsibility of the states, while the federal government is responsible for in-company nonschool training. The "social partners," principally employers and trade unions, have specified roles at every level of the system—national, regional, sectoral, company—principally through participation in an intricate web of advisory committees. The Chambers of Industry and Commerce, organized by occupational sector, have major responsibility for quality control in the system: they register apprenticeship contracts, supervise and monitor the quality of training in companies and training firms, assess the qualifications of VET trainers, and organize and carry out the final exams at the end of the apprenticeship period.

What is most striking to an American observer is the degree to which employers own responsibility for vocational education and training in the German system. This has deep historical and cultural roots in Germany, but it is also found in other systems, including Austria, Australia, the Netherlands, Norway, Denmark, Finland, and Switzerland. While tradition and strong cultural values undergird the continuing employer support for VET in Germany, enlightened self-interest is very much at work here as well. Simply put, German employers believe that the best way to get a highly qualified workforce is to invest in the development of young workers, participate directly in their training and socialization at the workplace, and then hire those who have proved themselves to be productive at the end of the apprenticeship period.

Because German workers are heavily unionized, it is very difficult and expensive to fire people once hired. Apprentices can be hired cheaply—typically, their wages in the third year are about half those of a regular new hire—and terminated easily if they don't work out. Swiss cost-benefit analyses have shown that productivity increases and other benefits contributed by apprentices more than offset the costs to employers, so it is not surprising that approximately one-quarter of all German employers choose to participate in the dual system, either by offering training places in their own firms or by contributing to intercompany training programs (a preferred option for very small companies).

Altogether, German employers in 2005 invested 27.7 billion euros in VET training costs, in contrast with governmental expenditures (national and state) of approximately 13.3 billion. While there is a downside to having a vocational education system so driven by employers, the other social partners, especially labor, provide a degree of balance; and the advantages of such a deep employer commitment to the development of young people cannot be overstated. While youth unemployment in the United States has reached epidemic proportions during the current economic downturn, young people in Germany continue to be employed at rates only modestly below those of adults.

I do not want to leave the impression that the German system is without flaws or problems. One negative consequence of their early tracking is that the young people in the bottom track—that is, the *Hauptschule*—leave school with weaker academic skills and consequently have a much more difficult time finding an apprenticeship than other students. For students who can't find an apprenticeship or a place in a full-time vocational school, Germany has established a bewildering number and variety of "transition" programs, on which it spends a great deal of money to produce relatively modest results. Approximately 15 percent of German young people opting for the VET pathway fail to obtain a labor market qualification by their midtwenties. Among young people who are labeled "migrants"—some of whom may in fact be children or grandchildren of people born in Germany—the numbers are much worse (36 percent without qualification). These are the same kinds of young people, of course, who fare worst in the United States.

I want to make two more points about the German system that should be of interest to the United States. The first has to do with basic education philosophy and, more particularly, with the dominant style of pedagogy in the VET system. Put simply, Germans believe that most people learn best by doing, and that academic concepts and skills are best developed in an applied context, where a young person has a chance to test out abstract ideas in a real-world situation. This view is very much present in the United States when we think about the training of professionals, where clinical practice or its equivalent is an essential component in the education of doctors, lawyers, architects, and (increasingly) teachers. When it comes to teenagers, however, we let them sit in classrooms all day although that is not how they are likely to learn best. If our young people have had difficulty in mastering basic literacy and numeracy skills by the time they enter high school, our answer is to give them double blocks of English and math. German vocational educators, by contrast, are died-in-the-wool progressives, keeping Dewey's ideas alive through their insistence that academic skills are best developed not by being taught separately but through embedding them in the presentation of complex workplace problems that students are expected to solve in the course of their part-time schooling. German educators also focus on helping students understand underlying theory—not just how things work, but why.

My final point about the German system is that, despite the early sorting and selection, the Germans have been working hard to build a stronger set of bridges connecting vocational and tertiary education. As I mentioned earlier, 17 percent of apprentices acquire an *Abitur* before choosing a VET program, signaling their understanding that having both sets of qualifications gives them a significant leg up in the labor market. This is but one path to combine academic and vocational preparation. For students who did not choose the *Gymnasium* option initially, some states now offer a pathway that enables *Realschule* graduates with a strong academic record to enroll in a more technically oriented *Gymnasium*, one that provides occupationally related instruction in engineering and technology fields and enables successful graduates to go on to tertiary education. This option is open to students who have completed an apprenticeship as well as those enrolling directly from lower secondary school. Another option for such students is to enroll in a *Fachobershule,* a school designed to prepare people for admission to universities of applied science. This is a one-year program for those who have a VET diploma, a two-year program for those enrolling with only a *Realschule* diploma. Finally, Germany is now beginning to see the dual-system philosophy extend into the university sector, where it is increasingly possible for enterprising students to combine work and learning in a semistructured way mirroring the VET system.

The big take-home message for me from Germany has less to do with the specifics of the institutional relationships that undergird the dual system and more to do with the underlying belief that from late adolescence onward, most young people learn best in structured programs that combine work and learning. This philosophy isn't simply about learning; it's also about how best to enable young people to make a successful transition "from initial education to working life," to cite the title of an earlier OECD report.[2] What is most striking about Germany is the investment, social as well as financial, that the society makes not only in supporting the development of the next generation of workers, but more generally in supporting the transition of young people from adolescence to adulthood. I am hardly unique in making this observation—it's the thesis of an excellent book on the German apprenticeship system by

Stephen Hamilton—but it suggests that if we could make progress in figuring out a viable American adaptation of the dual system, one that engages employers and educators in a much more collaborative approach to the education and training of the next generation of workers, it would likely produce an important set of social as well as economic returns on investment.[3]

4

Workplace Learning

"The School Is Not the Center of the World"

In many ways, the impulse to write this book came from my intense curiosity about how young people learn in the workplace.* Over the past few years, I have had the opportunity to visit a variety of apprenticeship sites across Europe. The results, when seen in a firm with students at work, are startling. In June 2008 and December 2010, I observed Norwegian apprentices in action at several companies— fish farming and solar panel sites above the Arctic Circle, a nursing home, and the leading Nordic company in Web development, communication solutions, and printing in Oslo. In September 2010, I visited BMW, which trains about forty apprentices a year in a spectacular plant in Leipzig, Germany, as well as two Swiss apprenticeship sites: Swisscom, the country's leading telecom provider, and BEKB/BCBE bank, a regional firm with 1,000 employees. Swisscom engages 813 apprentices chosen from among 7,000 applicants each year; the bank trains about 100 young people selected from among 700 applicants. As the BEKB/BCBE bank official explained, 10 percent of its workplaces are designed to be "educational." (For descriptions of these apprenticeship programs and to hear the voices of some young people and their

---

*This chapter's subtitle comes from *Report of SOMEC Coordinators on the Study Tour to Switzerland*, which reports on a visit of a group of Moldovan educators to learn about the Swiss VET system.

employers, see the journal essay "Ordinary Teenagers, Extraordinary Results.")

After my visits, I looked to the VET literature to supplement my own limited, admittedly nonrepresentative interviews and visits to apprentice workplaces. I wanted to know more about such questions as these: How are workplaces set up to be schoolhouses? When employers double as educators, what pedagogical techniques are used? What makes workplace learning as a requirement for the completion of upper secondary school different from merely learning on the job? I should have known that I would not find much research or even observational writing on this topic. There is research literature about worker, on-the-job training, and the occasional book of substantial literary quality about blue-collar occupations and the skills they require.[1] But these are much different endeavors than research into how sixteen- to nineteen-year-olds are introduced to the world of work and a career area while completing upper secondary schooling.

Traditional classrooms, let alone machine shop floors or banks or IT companies, are notoriously difficult sites for data collection and research. It is not only challenging but also slow and expensive to identify key variables across multiple locations over time and survey or observe widely enough to make generalizations. Thus, there is little observational or research literature on how teaching actually takes place in workplaces—what pedagogies are most effectively employed. As Yvonne Hillier, an expert on VET at the University of Brighton, rightly notes in one of the few recent articles on innovation in teaching and learning in vocational education, "Often people who are finding new and different ways to teach and help people learn do not publish what they are doing."[2]

To fill out the picture, I had to form an account indirectly. This chapter begins with a brief review of the most common kinds of workplace learning opportunities and the structures used for mounting the most intensive of them—apprenticeships and internships. It then moves on to discuss the challenges of workplace curriculum development, teaching, and assessment, and the training needed for mentoring young people at work. In the box "Work-Based Learning Versus Workplace Learning," I define these terms.

Work-Based Learning Versus Workplace Learning

The terminology of education and training can be confusing, especially when comparing the efforts in various countries, each employing its own lexicon. In this book, I try to make a consistent definitional distinction between work-based learning and workplace learning:

Work-*based* learning takes work as a subject of study and organizes curriculum around it. Some learning occurs in a workplace, but the main activities happen in schools. The learning is intended to provide the student with general knowledge about workplaces and often an introduction to specific careers, with the goal of helping teens to make appropriate career choices and encouraging them to continue their education. I would include under this term career and technical education (CTE), project-based learning, experiential learning, and various forms of applied learning.

Work*place* learning, as I use the term here, is delivered primarily in a work setting, with school-based instruction as a supplement or backdrop. It is structured and assessable, and ends in credit earned toward an occupational credential. One could say that *workplace learning* as I use it here is a subcategory of the much broader *work-based* learning arena.

CREATING A WORKPLACE LEARNING ENVIRONMENT

All workplace learning includes at least some student experience at a job. The type of work, the degree of supervision, and the amount of time involved vary by country, by program, and by partnering company. But all share practices that turn the workplace into a learning environment for teenagers. The main forms of workplace learning in which fifteen- to twenty-year-olds participate in the OECD countries include the following overlapping categories:

- *Job shadowing.* An experience where a student learns about a job by accompanying a worker through the day and observing workplace tasks and behaviors. Shadowing is temporary and unpaid, usually for younger students interested in exploring a particular career.

- *Service learning.* Voluntary work of an altruistic nature, often in nonprofit organizations, with the goals of helping the community and learning simultaneously. In the United States, service learning can be embedded in a college or high school course. This form of work-based learning with its ethic of volunteerism is mostly a U.S. phenomenon.

- *Internships.* Periods of work lasting weeks or months for low or no wages during which a student has the opportunity to learn a job by doing it. Outcomes may be governed by a special contract or a memorandum of understanding between a student and a company. In most countries, students in school-based upper secondary VET participate in internships, and increasingly internships are required in the technical and professional postsecondary institutions that have developed quickly in many strong VET countries. In formal terms, an internship is a period of supervised training required to qualify for a profession in a VET system. Most internships demand a specified number of academic credits or classroom years. In the United States, internships (also called clinical experiences or practica) are most common as a requirement in the health professions.

- *Apprenticeships.* Structured long-term workplace learning experiences with a wage and a contract created by a legal framework. Apprenticeships typically last several years and lead to a qualification or certification bestowed by an external body and valued as currency in the labor market. Most are company based, but some are primarily school based. Some countries have renamed apprenticeships in such fields as IT, social work, health, and finance as "modern apprenticeships" (United Kingdom) or traineeships (Australia, New Zealand) to signal that this type of extensive workplace learning is no longer only for the trades and manufacturing. (See figure 4.1 for a description of apprenticeships and traineeships in Queensland, Australia.)

- *Informal learning through part-time work.* In some countries, notably the United States, Australia, and the Netherlands, many students in upper secondary and tertiary education have part-time jobs. Although students work for financial reasons, they are likely to gain spin-off benefits of learning about work, the workplace, and work relationships.[3]

FIGURE 4.1 Apprenticeships and traineeships? What is the difference?

Apprenticeships are a long-standing system of combining training and employment so that people entering an occupation can receive instruction on specific skills while working in that particular occupation.

Apprenticeships are primarily of three to four years' duration and are at Certificate III or IV level. The apprentice enters into a training contract with the employer. Training is provided both on and off the job by the employer and a supervising registered training organization.

Apprenticeships in Australia have been mainly confined to skilled trade occupations, such as building and construction, engineering and metals, automotive. electrical and food trades.

Traineeships were introduced in 1985 to complement traditional apprenticeships by extending the coverage of "apprenticeship-type" training and employment to a much wider range of jobs across the whole labor market.

Traineeships are generally available at Certificate II level and above and can be anything from one year's duration up to three years or more. There are hundreds of traineeship vocations in a wide range of jobs across the whole labor market. As with an apprenticeship, the trainee enters into a training contract with the employer and training is provided both on and off the job by the employer and a supervising registered training organization.

Both school-based apprenticeships and school-based traineeships strengthen a young person's transition to further education, training and employment. The choice of a school-based apprenticeship or school-based traineeship will be informed by the industry in which the young person is seeking to work, their aptitudes and other learning and employment goals.

Source: Adapted from *School-Based Apprenticeships and Traineeships: The Queensland Government Agenda* (Queensland Department of Education, Training and Arts, n.d.), http://www.apprenticeshipsinfo.qld.gov.au/resources/sats-policy.pdf.

Another useful way to categorize workplace learning within non-U.S. vocational education is by the proportion of time spent in school versus in a company. *Learning for Jobs* labels as an apprenticeship or a dual system one in which students spend at least 60 percent of their weekly learning time at a company. The workplace, not the school, is the center of their world. Often called alternance arrangements, continuous dual-system training involves one or two days of schooling in a VET institution and three or four days of training and working in a company throughout the two to four years of apprenticeship training.

Table 4.1 shows the extent to which countries use workplace learning in their vocational programs. In some countries, almost all vocational students receive extensive training in a real work environment. In other countries, different amounts and sequences of workplace learning are available from full apprenticeships to learning for jobs in school.

Some countries—notably Norway—structure their apprenticeship systems with two years of schooling followed by two years of work experience. Some occupations require substantial theoretical and practical training before an apprentice is able to do meaningful work. Thus, in some systems, apprentices spend months, or years, in a VET institution or in specialized training centers before starting to work in a company. In addition, some systems tailor apprenticeships according to two additional criteria: how long it takes to train for a particular occupation, and how long a student wants to be in training before she or he becomes a regular employee. For example, in the Netherlands, students may choose VET programs lasting from one to four years, with the longer programs leading to tertiary VET and to managerial training.

A training organization, rather than a company or a school, may deliver some of the work-related training. For example, in Switzerland, occupational sectors organize training in practical skills to be delivered to groups of students from different companies at a training organization. Australia makes substantial use of registered training organizations, known as *RTOs*, to deliver components of VET education.

Workplace learning can be carried out in weekly, monthly, or yearly blocks—or may be only a minor aspect of school-based VET, such as in the Swedish fifteen-week work experience. But the strongest systems combine some school and some workplace learning either each week or in blocks of several weeks. Both Sweden and Norway are considering alterations to their systems to get closer to that model. Sweden's school-based VET system currently mounts a fifteen-week work placement for each student during their three years of VET education, but the placements are not consistently available. Students take part where partner companies can be found with relative ease. As of 2009, however, Sweden has moved to require a work placement, and will limit student places in programs if no placements are available. In addition, Sweden is planning to implement a pilot apprenticeship

TABLE 4.1 Time spent by VET students in work placements

Estimated percentage of secondary VET students, by time spent in work placement (as ratio of the total program length)

Percent of program length spent in work placement with employers

	75% or more	Between 50% and 75%	Between 25% and 50%	Less than 25%
Australia[1]	■■	—	—	—
Austria	■■	—	—	■■■
Belgium (FI)[1]	■	—	—	—
Czech Republic	—	—	—	■■■■
Denmark	—	■■■■	—	—
Finland	■	—	—	■■■■
France	■	—	—	■■■
Germany[2]	—	■■■	—	■
Netherlands	—	■■	■■■	—
Norway[2]	—	■■■■	—	—
Sweden[2]	—	—	—	■■■
Switzerland	■	■■■■	—	—
United States	—	—	—	■■■■

Note: Estimated percentage of VET secondary programs: — 0%; ■ 1–25%; ■■ 26–50%; ■■■ 51–75%; ■■■■ 76–100%.

[1]In Australia, Belgium (Flanders), and Switzerland the amount of workplace training depends on the institution and program.

[2]Some missing data, so not all programs are represented.

Source: Recreated from OECD, *Learning for Jobs: OECD Reviews of Vocational Education and Training* (Paris: OECD Publishing, 2010), table 5.1, http://dx.doi.org/10.1787/9789264087460-en. Used with permission.

program starting in 2011.[4] To create stronger linkages between school and work, the Oslo school authority is building a new school that is designed to integrate school and work, an experiment that would abandon Norway's long used two-plus-two system—two years of VET in school followed by two years of apprenticeship, with the fourth year as a full employee of the training company.

The most effective systems offer firms the flexibility to choose the program best suited to their needs. The ability to decide the duration of the apprenticeship is one factor important to both employers and students: it helps ensure that apprentices reach their training objectives and that employer costs and benefits are in balance. For example, Swiss research has demonstrated that the time required to reach a given level of productivity varies, depending on the skills requirements of different occupations and the aptitudes and talents of the student.[5] Australia has abolished its time-based assessment system in favor of a competency-based system. Motivated students now can acquire skills quickly; they can move through training at their own pace.

"HEAD, HEART, AND HAND": TEACHING TO DEVELOP COGNITIVE, AFFECTIVE, AND PRACTICAL CAPACITIES

Given the many attractive aspects of an education that teaches occupational skills and knowledge, nurturing a carefully crafted combination of capacities—cognitive, affective, and practical—in school and in the workplace, the reader likely will be asking, how does learning actually take place, especially when students attend two different sites with different teachers, and sometimes a third site (when a training organization is involved)? To start sorting out the issues, one must distinguish between what one would want to know about school-based learning from what one would want to know about the workplace from a third question—how are school and workplace integrated? For school, the goal is to ensure that students learn the basics—reading, writing, math, history, languages, and often the theory behind career applications. For workplaces, the goal is the application of skills and knowledge, and the development of competence. Much of school-based teaching and learning goes on in traditional ways, although where workplace learning is fully problem based, there are reflections back in the school curriculum. That is, the workplace, not the school, is the center of the student's world of learning, and the school reflects workplace needs, not vice versa. As some Moldovan visitors to the Swiss education system observed in their report on the visit, "'The school is not the center of the world'; it is just a service-providing institution that should meet the client's needs. The future apprentices think less about which school to go to and more about learning an occupation in order to . . . get a good job."[6]

The challenge is teaching to support learning in the workplace. If students do not learn just by being given a job and some supervision, how then should they be taught? How are reading, writing, and math improved while a student is on the job? Especially important, how are the so-called people skills—the nontangible attitudes and behaviors required for work success—developed?

In most VET systems, outcomes, as noted above, are codified as skills, knowledge, and competencies called qualifications. But creating curriculum, designing learning activities, and preparing people to teach and train in the workplace should not be confused with specifying outcomes. To characterize the teaching and learning challenge, we find it useful to begin with vignettes of the kind of skills, knowledge, and competencies students should develop, but articulated as employers describe them, rather than as they appear in curriculum or translated into competency statements. For example, in a conference paper that addresses the "the aim and challenge of vocational schools . . . to integrate theoretical contents and workplace-orientated applications," Daniela Moser, an Austrian researcher, asked professionals how they act in standard work situations.[7] Good vocational education curriculum development and teaching strategies begin with such "real-time" observations. Moser explains:

> The scope of vocational standard situations comprises diverse scenarios like client counseling, order handling, construction, handling means of work and products, planning and repair work. The tasks described were information providing, product calculations, engineering changes, troubleshooting and starting up machines. Organizational tasks are organization of internal processes, materials procurement and taking over new functions. Furthermore, fields of handling were defined, such as complaint handling. This implies adequate behavior, like exercising patience and empathy, taking up

personal distance and finding solutions, but also objective argumentation. In other examples, the necessity of deviations from "normal" ways of acting is asked for as well as using professional knowledge and experience, the search for new motivation, readiness for working overtime. Of utmost importance seems to be the initiative to co-operate and communicate.

Another example refers to the necessity of calling on experts; this seemed to be important for further learning activities, which is a crucial requirement for flexible employees. In some cases customer and employee have differing opinions about the scale of benefits so it is necessary to find a connection between communicative abilities and professional knowledge. Professional knowledge is important to submit warranty claims and communicative abilities are basic to inform the customers. Structured ability to reason is a crucial resource . . . [for] defect detection and troubleshooting. In cases of errors and bad workmanship it is necessary to make short-term modifications in the production flow, therefore flexible organizational handling is demanded. Management functions include planning of staff and other resources. Personal adaptability like finding compromises is essential to come to fair solutions in assigning new functions.[8]

Several decades ago, to prepare young people for the workplace, many VET systems began to shift policy and practice to phase out discipline-based instruction in schools in favor of an approach built from real problems young people must solve in the workplace, such as those outlined above from Moser's employer interviews. Recounting this transformation, two researchers report, in Germany, school curricula for vocational education and training in a particular occupation were traditionally derived from corresponding academic disciplines (e.g., engineering sciences or economic sciences), while curricula for in-company training were produced in a bargaining process between the social partners, guided by ministries and the German National Institute of Vocational Education and Training (BIBB). The trend to drive education toward application of knowledge and away from acquisition alone responded to complaints from employers that students and their teachers and trainers had difficulty translating what was learned into practice. For example, taking a course on electrophysics did not mean a student could repair a car; completing a course in physiology did not enable a student to provide physical care for an elderly patient in a nursing home. Such complaints about gaps between theory and practice, linking school-based and workplace learning, emerged among students and employers in many occupations. The revision of commercial training in Switzerland, described in chapter 3, began with a similar set of employer complaints that training was too academic, too little focused on helping young people become autonomous decision makers and problem solvers who could reflect on their learning and self-correct.

The challenge in VET pedagogy today is to build curriculum and assessments that replicate authentically the uncertain, messy, problem-based, people-intense, and time-limited world of work. The German researchers cited above describe curriculum derived from what are called *learning areas*: VET teachers must "identify *occupational situations* which are significant for the work activity and also have a potential for learning."[9] To develop such learning situations entails a complex series of steps, beginning with analysis of work activity and the required competences, followed by the development of work process–related and competence-based curricula, and ending with the design of work process–related learning situations. An Australian researcher, Jane Figgis, says students should learn "in a way that does not disrupt (or only very minimally disrupts) the regular pattern of work (and this goal) takes him/her into new and difficult terrain."[10] The Swiss Federal Institute for VET has a unit devoted to the process of analyzing work situations, breaking them into their component activities and problems, and developing representative competencies and curricula (see chapter 2).

The seriousness with which the Germanic countries, in particular, take the challenge of applied learning is exemplified by the degree to which even foundational skills—reading, writing, and mathematics—are embedded into technical and occupational skill development. In Germany and Austria, students spend only 160 hours per year in "regular" school. This is a strategy not without challenges. The OECD studies of both countries cite employer concerns about the quality of basic skills of young people starting their apprenticeships, confirmed by mediocre test scores.[11] School officials note that VET teachers and trainers do not have expertise in teaching basic skills nor in diagnosing problems. Given that concerns of this kind are pervasive among employers in most countries, it is hard to point to the embedding of skills as the source of the problem; and it is significant that the Germans are adamant about making it work rather than taking math and writing back to the classroom.

The Swiss curricula are occupation specific, and for each occupation, four steps are taken:

1. Selection of subjects (e.g., some occupations have mandatory foreign language learning, others chemistry)

2. Weighting of the share of each subject during the duration of the apprenticeship

3. Selection of issues taught within a subject (e.g., mathematics is not taught according to the same canon of sub-subjects as in academic schooling; some occupations require more trigonometry, others calculus, others more algebra)

4. Definition of the responsibilities of VET schools and the training companies

Such decisions follow the general principle that topics or subjects that do not require practical application or can be taught more effectively and cost-efficiently in a school setting should be delegated to schools, and vice versa. The schools are also crucial learning environments for giving every apprentice the chance to learn with similar quality and intensity while quality and intensity varies within companies. Thus, the learning delegated to schools also plays a part in guaranteeing equal chances in learning outcomes.

But independent of whether the subject is taught at school or at the workplace, teachers use pedagogy and examples that are related to the occupation. For example, Switzerland develops curriculum tailored to each occupation: mathematics for technical occupations, for commercial occupations, and recently for cooks.[12]

The point is that however executed—and sometimes not to the desired standard—the informing orientation of VET (sometimes required by statute) is authentic, problem- rather than discipline-based learning. In a study entitled "Regenerating the Australian Landscape of Professional VET Practice," Figgis identified the following trends characterizing effective VET teachers: "using authentic learning tasks as the basis for learning; encouraging peer learning; applying e-learning technologies; using the workplace as the primary site for learning and skill development; personalizing learning; and devolving support for teaching and learning so that it is close to the practitioner.[13]

If this sounds to American readers like a combination of project- and competency-based learning, those would be appropriate reference points. But it is important to note that a number of analysts explicitly reject a narrow view of competence as a set of work-related skills— as do the most effective training sites—a point that I discuss at some length in chapter 1 in the section on the distinctions between job training and learning for a calling or vocation. Using the language of constructivism, these analysts see the U.S. attempt in the 1960s to implement competency-based education as a failure because the units of learning were too small and too behaviorist, and resulted in fragmented rather than holistic learning. Competencies, most would argue, must be linked together; they are interdependent. Analysts and researchers prefer the language of communities of practice; they cite Jean Lave and Etienne Wenger's theory of situated learning as the presiding spirit of their pedagogical approaches, both in school and in companies. Those focused on pedagogy tend to emphasize not the specific technical skills but the ability "to gain competences, which enable [the learner] . . . to act autonomously in complex and unpredictable situations."[14]

Increasingly, strong VET systems are teaching the kinds of knowledge, skills, and competencies recommended, for example, by the U.S. economists Richard Murnane and Frank Levy, in which they divided the tasks carried out by U.S. workers into five categories:

Expert thinking. Solving problems for which there are no rule-based solutions

Complex communication. Interacting with others to acquire information, to explain it, or to persuade others of its implications for action
Routine cognitive tasks. Mental tasks that are well described by logical rules
Routine manual tasks. Physical tasks that can be well described using rules
Nonroutine manual tasks. Physical tasks that cannot be well described as following a set of "if-then do" rules and that are difficult to computerize[15]

Of these, they argue, computers cannot replicate expert thinking and complex communication, and thus making them subjects to be taught and practiced is critical to providing young people will skills, knowledge, and competencies that cannot be easily off shored or automated.

In her interviews with Australian VET teachers, Figgis looks for those who are teaching through authentic tasks that capture a number of the categories above. In her definition, "authentic tasks . . . are different from simply practical tasks. An authentic task not only has real-world relevance (a context which reflects the way the skill and knowledge will be used in real life), but it needs to be a complex task completed over a sustained period of time, over days, weeks, even months, rather than minutes or hours." She cites Mihaly Csikszentmihalyi's notion of "flow activity or an optimal experience . . . [where] there is a perfect balance between the challenge set by an activity and the 'stretch' required to achieve it. If the stretch is too great (the challenge too hard), the person gives up. If the task is too easy (no stretch required), the task is just boring. But if the balance is set just right and the activity delivers ongoing feedback on how the person is progressing, then the activity will be fully engaging." As an example, she describes changes made to the required daily journal for apprentices at Blue Dog Training in Queensland, an award-winning RTO that was recognized for its "custom-designed interactive, animation-rich learning resources and quizzes which learners complete online during work down time."[16] (See figure 4.2.)

While the description of authentic tasks is a piece of the puzzle, it does not tell us much about how actual teaching in the workplace over

FIGURE 4.2 Construction Apprentices: Blue Dog Training

Blue Dog Training was set up in 2005 by three TAFE lecturers who believed that construction training could be done better and more flexibly—that apprentices needn't ever come into a TAFE institute. So the apprentices do all their practice within the authentic domain of their employer and study Blue Dog's comprehensive materials during the employer's downtime.

The interesting "authentic task" is Blue Dog's electronic logbook, which has become a central and invigorating feature of its training. "Filling in paper-and-pencil logbooks," according to Kris Andre [director of Blue Dog Training, which won the 2009 Innovative Business Award of the Australian Training Awards in 2009], "where apprentices are expected to write down each day what they did and how it applies to each unit is probably the least authentic and greatest drudge of the normal apprenticeship experience. There are many units, and tasks sometimes apply to several units, and the apprentices have to sort it all out."

The apprentices do have to enter what they've done into the electronic logbook, but much of the cumbersome repetition has been removed. What makes it an "authentic task" is:

- The scope for apprentices to add all sorts of artifacts to the logbook, not least snapshots of the work they've completed (and of themselves at work) taken with their mobile phones.

- The short quizzes embedded in the logbook (and behind each question there may be six or twelve variations), so if the apprentice gets a question wrong, the next time it is asked in a different way. And they can't go on until they've got it right. Further, if the apprentice hasn't made an entry about practical work for a week, they are automatically locked out of the theory part.

- The system generates on-site evaluation of a whole range of reports for licensing, for employers: the apprentices' whole work history is there, and when employers see that with the pictures and all, they are very impressed.

Source: Jane Figgis, "Regenerating the Australian Landscape of Professional VET Practice: Practitioner-Driven Changes to Teaching and Learning," *A National Vocational Education and Training Research and Evaluation Program Report* (Adelaide, Australia: NCVER, 2009).

weeks or months actually goes on. An excellent entrée into the topic comes not from Europe or Australia, but from the United States, Norton Grubb's 1999 study of occupational instruction in community colleges. Grubb observed and interviewed 114 occupational instructors in 23 schools. While he focused on U.S. settings, his characterization of the complexity of occupational teaching could describe the challenge before most VET teachers and trainers. In addition to cognitive skills, Grubb notes that "in most occupations there are many competencies to master including manual and visual abilities, problem-solving and interpersonal skills as well as conventional linguistic and mathematical abilities." He points out that while there is a vast literature on teaching and learning in math, writing, or reading, there is almost none on the greater challenges of honing students' manual dexterity or helping them develop mental and visual skills demanded by three-dimensional spaces required in engineering or auto mechanics. Even for more traditional school skills like reading, Grubb notes, students encounter a wide array of nonacademic texts: manuals, diagrams, maps, invoices, spreadsheets, blueprints, and the like. Not only do these require specialized reading and interpretation skills, they also often are authoritative in a way literary texts are not. In some regulated professions, there is only one right way to do something.[17]

Grubb distinguishes between teaching "skills" and teaching "systems," or what many call today *systems thinking*. He gives two examples of the systems approach:

> The difference was nicely illustrated by an auto instructor. In the approach he has refused to take, time is divided into small units like academic classes—"kowtowing to the academics"—where each unit is devoted to a particular sub-skill. This instructor considers the "skills" approach to be a failure. His approach has been to have longer classes where students work on real projects—cars with different problems—where students learn by having them "get on the cars and mess around." In this problem-driven approach, technical skills are learned by developing solutions to larger problems—whole-to-part instruction rather than part-to-whole. While he describes the workshop as "messing around," he structures the problems—the cars that come in—so that students rotate through all-important automotive systems.[18]

Grubb described the instructor's effort to "get away from the shop environment": "We wanted to get away from the manual training, specific, narrowly focused, 'here's how a pump works' environment to 'let's look at the hydraulics fundamentals involved here, let's look at pneumatics, let's look at applied physics, let's look at applied mathematics'—not just cars, but the entire concept of hydraulics . . . I try to teach them how things work, you know, the theory behind—like how an automatic transmission works."[19]

In the second example, Grubb describes the higher quality of instruction in drafting when it is taught not as a motor skill, but rather as a problem in visualization that entails moving from three- to two-dimensional representation. In the skills approach, "the result is often a copying exercise where students use board or CAD to copy drawings, rather than thinking about the process of two-dimensional representation."[20]

Finally, an enormously important aspect of workplace learning concerns social, communication, and teamwork skills. The capacity to convey such skills involves more than the ability to exercise them. That is, a supervisor can calm an angry client, but that doesn't mean she can teach a young person what to do in a confrontation. A study from Australia found that apprentices highly valued the social skills of supervisors, such as communication skills and the capacity to deal with conflicts, but that many supervisors felt they lacked the skills to respond to their apprentices' expectations. A study from the United Kingdom found that supervisors without specific training tend to focus on occupation-specific skills and neglect broader social competences.[21] This area could be an important topic for further research. In my observations, such skills are taught more by the supervisor's behaving as a role model than by an aspect of the curriculum.

Assessment

Teaching through authentic tasks—designing a task-based instructional system as distinct from a content-based one—makes new and quite challenging demands on practitioners. It is no small order to come up with tasks that are simultaneously effective in generating the requisite learning and achievable by the learners and deeply engaging. Further, learners themselves often need to be led gradually to this new way of learning. Practitioners report that it often takes several attempts before the approach works relatively predictably, and even then new learner cohorts or new bright ideas from the learners themselves mean that readjustments, both minor and major, may be required.[22]

A significant lever for the integration of school and workplace learning is achieved when final assessments are designed and administered by the school and social partners together and require the integration of skills and knowledge as applied to authentic problems.[23] Both Norway and the Netherlands have single applied exams produced locally but aligned with national qualifications to specific standards of quality within each occupation. The Norwegian exam at the end of the two years of school and two years of apprenticeship is characterized as a practical-theoretical trade and journeyman's examination lasting several days. Switzerland has a particularly well-respected assessment system directed by a national assessment board and involving the social partners, VET schools, and cantonal offices. (See figure 4.3 for an example of how disciplinary learning is incorporated.)

An additional dimension of the commitment to holistic, or systems, teaching and learning concerns the use of modularized curriculum. A number of countries have moved to modularize components of the curriculum both to enable efficiencies in teaching common core subjects that are required for a number of trades or careers, and to enable students to customize their specializations. The key to maintaining a focus on the parts and the whole together appears in the manner by which skills and knowledge are assessed. In its employer-controlled system, England, for example—with its focus on preparation for specific tasks at the expense of the broader shaping of a calling or career—assesses modules separately, while VET systems in other countries teach in modular fashion, but credit is determined by assessment of the completed qualification; no credits or certificates are given for modules, in order to maintain the status of a given profession.[24]

VET Teachers and Trainers

The strong VET countries, as well as the United States, face the looming retirement of many CTE teachers, who are best equipped to train the replacement teacher corps (see the box "CTE Teacher Preparation in the United States"). With their commitment to workplace learning,

FIGURE 4.3   Final VET exams in Switzerland

In Switzerland, apprentices have to pass a formal exam to obtain a VET qualification (*Eidgenössisches Berufsattest*) in the end of a 2-year apprenticeship or *Eidgenössisches Fähigkeitszeugnis* in the end of 3–4-year apprenticeships). The formal exam is national and takes place at the same point in time for all students. Some regional variation (between the German-, French- and Italian-speaking parts of the country) is however possible.

The assessment has several elements. The exam is organized by a national examination board, which is composed of representatives from VET schools, social partners, and cantonal VET offices under the control of the cantons. The exam can take place either in the part-time VET school, the workplace, or a workshop (*Ausbildungszentren für überbetriebliche Kurse*). It is composed of a written and an oral part; both are supervised and carried out by experts designated by the cantons.

The apprentices have to carry out a piece of practical work (either a simulation of everyday work-life situation or the end-of-study project, *Gesellenstück*) and answer questions on occupation-specific knowledge and general knowledge (in the field of language and society, including economics, legal knowledge, or ecology). The exam tasks on occupation-specific knowledge are developed by the social partners, while those on general knowledge are prepared and examined by the VET schools. The final mark is typically composed as follows: the practical work counts 40%, the occupation-specific tasks 20%, general knowledge 20%, and the average of all the marks in the part-time VET school counts another 20%. All results are taken together at the examination board, which also publishes the formal results.

Source: Adapted from *Learning for Jobs, OECD Reviews of Vocational Education and Training* (Paris: OECD Publishing, 2010). Used with permission.

they think differently than U.S. educators about how teachers should enter a system of education that has had a long partnership with industry and a tradition of differentiating roles for school instructors and VET instructors. They understand that preparation for career and tertiary education is not the job of a single educator.

Within the strong VET systems, many more people than in school-based learning are formally and informally involved in the transmission of vocational skills and knowledge. *Learning for Jobs* makes a distinction between vocational *trainers* as those, whether in VET institutions or workplaces, who are primarily responsible for imparting practical

CTE Teacher Preparation in the United States

In the United States, over the last decade the role of CTE teachers has changed significantly from preparing young people for a specific first job right after high school to preparing students for a range of occupations, as well as for postsecondary education—whether a short-term credential or a college degree. CTE teachers, many of whom are nearing retirement age, were not trained for this array of challenges. For all teachers, and especially those in CTE, college and career readiness represents a substantial advance in academic proficiency. In addition, since CTE is no longer primarily about specialization—that is the role of community college occupational and technical programs—CTE teachers must now have knowledge not only of a specific occupation, but also about the world of work in general. To add to these demands, twenty-first-century skills—the ability to communicate, to work in teams, to problem solve—are more visibly linked to CTE programs than to college prep.

As the CTE standards from the National Board for Professional Teaching Standards note, the accomplished CTE teacher should "command a core body of knowledge about the world of work in general and the skills and processes that cut across industries, industry-specific knowledge, and a base of general academic knowledge. They draw on this knowledge to establish curricular goals, design instruction, facilitate student learning, and assess student progress."[a]

Since that statement was written in 1997, the demand for workers with high-level technical skills has grown, putting additional demands on the CTE teacher. While the United States does not have nationally recognized qualifications required for entry into the majority of occupations, industry standards, licenses (issues by states) and certifications do exist—and their numbers are growing. High schools want to offer some of them, so teachers whose students are working toward certification or licensure in automotive

vocational skills, and vocational *teachers* as those who are primarily responsible for theoretical vocational skills. VET institutions also employ *general education teachers* who are responsible for general subjects, such as mathematics, economics, or second languages. In practice, the boundaries are often blurred and sometimes deliberately. In Norway, for example, the teaching of theoretical and practical vocational skills is increasingly combined in the two years of school–based vocational or IT or a health field must stay up to date on requirements and be able to incorporate industry standards into the curriculum.[b]

The transformation of the requirements for teaching in a CTE program has been accompanied by the decline in the number of postsecondary institutions offering CTE teacher education credentialing and a rise in admission standards for those programs. CTE teachers can gain certification in two ways: through a teacher education program leading to a BA, and through alternative certification. With the decline in BA slots, alternative certification has grown. While alternatively certified teachers come from industry and thus have substantial knowledge of a particular occupation, they need not have BA degrees, although some candidates do. Neither the BA holders nor those solely from industry will have had any training in pedagogy, however. The non-BA holders may struggle to teach to the rising academic standards. To become certified, alternative candidates need only complete a small number of education courses. In a study of twelve thousand CTE teachers at High Schools That Work (HSTW) sites in thirty states, researchers found that around 75 percent of CTE teachers had entered through the alternative route.[c]

In short, the United States faces a challenge in providing an extensive and well-trained CTE teaching force to carry out the many complex tasks now in CTE job descriptions.

[a]National Board for Professional Teaching Standards, *Career and Technical Education Standards*, 1997,13, http://www.nbpts.org/userfiles/File/eaya_cte_standards.pdf.
[b]James R. Stone III, *Professional Development for Secondary Career and Technical Education: Implications for Change*, (Louisville, KY: National Research Center for Career and Technical Education, 2010), 32.
[c]Gene Bottoms and K. McNally, *Actions States Can Take to Place a Highly Qualified Career/Technical Teacher in Every Classroom* (Atlanta, GA: Southern Regional Education Board, 2005).

education before the apprenticeship. In Austria, Germany, and Switzerland, general subjects (e.g., sciences) are often adapted to and embedded in the relevant vocational field (e.g., science for electricians).

A major challenge to school-based VET is ensuring that trainers are familiar with the fast-changing requirements of modern workplaces. In many countries, there are staff who work part-time as trainers and part-time in industry. Such arrangements offer particular benefits because these trainers remain in close touch with the changing needs of the modern workplace, and this pattern of working may also appeal to those who wish to develop a career as a trainer but retain a job in industry. Skilled workers may also be hired from companies on short-term contracts to fill trainer vacancies. Such arrangements exist in Norway and Sweden, where VET institutions and local employers cooperate to ensure an adequate supply of vocational trainers. In Sweden, the *Learning for Jobs* team visited a twenty-first-century Saab repair facility shared with, and adjacent to, a school. The technicians used the facility with students as apprentices three days a week and two days on their own for regular business.

The qualifications required to practice as a teacher/trainer vary among OECD countries, with requirements in many countries (e.g., Korea) being higher for vocational teachers than for trainers. General education teachers—for example, those teaching physics to electricians in VET institutions—are in a somewhat different position. While workplace experience may be less relevant to them than to their colleagues responsible for practical skills, there remain issues about both the content of what is taught (so that it is most useful in the workplace) and how it is taught (so that its relevance is clear to the student).

In Switzerland, teachers of these general subjects in VET institutions are required to take an additional course to ensure that the subjects are made relevant to the needs of VET students. To qualify, candidates must already have a teaching credential and teaching experience, and work in a profession. They then enter a modularized two-year training program. For those who already have a teacher's certificate at the upper secondary level, this involves three hundred learning hours. The institution that commonly provides these courses (see figure 4.4) also serves as a center of expertise and research on the training of VET teachers and trainers, and in the professional training of VET administrators.

Preparing Industry Trainers

While VET institutions often want to improve their trainers' familiarity with the workplace, the concern in industry is more often to equip the supervisors of apprentices and trainees with pedagogical skills. Supervisors play a key role: they pass on practical skills, but also transmit

---

FIGURE 4.4 The Swiss Federal Institute for Vocational Education and Training

---

The Swiss Federal Institute for Vocational Education and Training (SFIVET) is the national competency center for teaching and research in vocational and professional education and training (VET/PET). SFIVET has regional campuses in three of Switzerland's linguistic regions. Its activities encompass basic and continuing training of vocational teachers and trainers as well as research and development for the government and professional associations.

SFIVET's **Basic Training Division** provides training to full-time and part-time teachers working at vocational schools and professional colleges, as well as to other VET/PET professionals. The master of science (MSc) degree program in vocational education and training provides university graduates with the opportunity to gain academic qualifications in the VET/PET field.[a]

SFIVET's **Continuing Training Division** offers continuing education and training courses designed to upgrade the skills of VET/PET professionals; enable VET organizations to develop their activities; provide VET/PET managers with advanced training; and promote quality and innovation within the Swiss VET/PET system.

SFIVET's **Research and Development Division** explores and lays the foundations for basic and continuing training in the VET/PET field. In particular, it carries out evaluations and impact assessments or develops competency measurement concepts that serve as the basis for further VET/PET developments.

SFIVET mainly pursues applied research questions in the VET/PET field. It works closely with universities and other research institutes in Switzerland and abroad. The Research and Development Division is also responsible for assessing and monitoring the quality of the training programs and courses as well as the quality of consulting and development services provided by SFIVET.

[a]See http://www.ehb-schweiz.ch/en/training/degreeprogrammes/Pages/allgmeinbildenderunterrichtanberufsfachschulen.aspx.

Source: Federal Office for Professional Education and Technology, Vocational and Professional Education and Training in Switzerland, national report from Switzerland contributing to the OECD's review, Learning for Jobs (Bern: Federal Office for Professional Education and Technology, 2008).

---

theoretical knowledge, help apprentices and trainees get used to the social codes of the workplace, and, more broadly, are responsible for the management of apprentices and trainees.

Evidence from various countries suggests that when apprentice supervisors receive specific training, they do a better job of developing the skills of apprentices. In Australia, workplace trainers found specific training courses helpful in developing supervising competences.

In Germany, the suspension of compulsory training for workplace trainers seems to have had a negative impact on the quality of apprenticeships. This requirement was suspended for five years, as firms complained that it was a barrier to their offering apprenticeships, and it has only recently been reintroduced. The first evaluations of the suspension show that in companies without qualified training staff, apprentice dropout rates were higher, and companies complained more about the performance of their apprentices. The social partners associated the suspension with a deterioration in the image and quality of VET. Both training and nontraining companies considered formal requirements for workplace trainers as a guarantee of minimum standards. Training for workplace trainers may also have spillover benefits, since the competences acquired by trainers tend to be shared within the company. This is particularly important, since regular colleagues also contribute to the learning experience of apprentices by answering questions, showing apprentices how to perform tasks, or providing informal feedback.[25]

In most OECD countries, relevant work experience is necessary to become a trainer, but trainers are less often expected to have pedagogical training or develop management competences. Some of these latter requirements can be found in countries with strong apprenticeship systems, including Austria, Germany, and Switzerland. Figure 4.5 gives two examples of trainer preparation.

In some countries, trainers in VET institutions work temporarily in companies to update their vocational competences. In Australia, links between VET colleges (TAFEs) and companies have fostered mutual understanding and exchange of knowledge. Often the quality of such partnerships depends heavily on personal relationships, and while such relationships are important, they need to be systematically supported.

CONCLUSION

Most educators and business leaders in the United States—and CTE educators, most certainly—would agree that some form of work-based learning should be included in students' pathways. Nonetheless, very

FIGURE 4.5 Preparation of vocational trainers in companies

In **Belgium-Flanders**, employers who take apprentices receive 12 hours of training, called "Estafette." The program focuses on issues such as welcoming apprentices, giving instructions and feedback, and conflict management. This training is compulsory for all new employers and supervisors, and for existing employers and supervisors who seek a relaxation of some element of regulation or have faced problems with apprentices.

In **Switzerland**, firms need to meet quality standards supervised by the canton in order to take apprentices. Apprentice supervisors must complete a 100-hour training course, which includes pedagogy, legal issues, knowledge of the VET system, and potential problems with young people such as drugs or alcohol. As part of the quality assurance process, cantonal inspectors interview apprentices and employees in the company to monitor the quality of training. In case of a problem, the canton provides some "coaching" to the company. The companies recognize the benefits of this approach, as well-trained apprentices will have a stronger productive contribution.

Source: Recreated from OECD, *Learning for Jobs: OECD Reviews of Vocational Education and Training* (Paris: OECD Publishing, 2010), box 2.8, http://dx.doi.org/10.1787/9789264087460-en. Used with permission.

few CTE programs or academic high schools have work-based learning opportunities that resemble in any way those in the strong VET countries. In the United States, work-based learning opportunities are not standardized or available to all who want them, nor is quality evaluated against accepted criteria. For the average high school student in a vocational program, internships are scattershot, and work-based experiences of any depth and extent are the exception, not the rule. U.S. schools do not have systematized connections with employers, nor do employers see it in their self-interest to provide work-based learning. Absent a mainstream system built to put young people into workplaces—and one that demands the assessment of students' ability to solve multidimensional and unpredictable problems that people encounter at work as a measure of competence—the United States will not make much progress in promoting workplace learning.

In the United States today, we have only one mainstream system—and that is the "college for all" route. There is no clearly defined second mainstream route that young people can choose if they wish to start on learning for a career at age sixteen. The countries profiled in this book have two systems—VET and an academic track—and the former provides the middle-skilled, entry-level employees who can fuel economic growth and go on to strengthen their skills and expertise as the needs of the economy change. While none of these countries would discount the significance of a well-trained research and professional sector, they are increasingly agnostic about how such highly skilled and creative people arrive at their destinations. For the majority of young people, these countries have come to conclude that starting off in the workplace is healthy for young people, and a support—not a limit—to their development.

Ordinary Teenagers, Extraordinary Results

Apprentices at Work

By Nancy Hoffman

In a small office lined with desks and computer stations, a dozen teenagers pored over paperwork and deliberated decisions, one young man zipping from table to table in a wheelchair. The young people, sixteen to eighteen years old, were reading, discussing, and evaluating job applications. On other days, they attended secondary school. But for more than half of each week, they worked—as apprentices here at Swisscom, Switzerland's largest telecommunications company. Their current role was in human resources, determining who would be invited to sit for the five-hour exam that begins the process of selecting next year's Swisscom apprentices.

I was visiting Swisscom to learn more about its remarkable apprenticeship program. The first thing these student workers told me, proudly, is that earning a spot there is highly competitive. (About one in twelve applicants are accepted.) Their supervisor, a burly, smiling man in jeans and a T-shirt, asked a duo examining an application folder to explain how they made their initial judgments.

A German-speaking young man and his French-speaking female partner told me—in English—the gist of the cover letter they had under review, pointing out the one grammatical error they had marked in red. They had examined school grades, test results, and teacher recommendations, particularly the teacher's enthusiasm about the student's values and ability to get along with others. This candidate did not make the cut; the school grades were not great at the beginning of lower secondary school and had not risen sufficiently to demonstrate growth. "Do you like doing this work?" I asked. Big smiles all around. "I'm here for six months in this project," the young woman said. "Then I apply for a different project to learn other competencies. This one's really fun and interesting." "How old are you?" I asked, impressed with her poise. "Sixteen," she said.

In September 2010, I toured Swisscom and a second commercial enterprise in Bern, a regional bank known as BEKB/BCBE. A main function of each company—along with many other Swiss firms—is training the country's next generation of workers. I had caught a glimpse of similar programs before, but I wanted to learn more. The previous year, as part of expert teams assembled by OECD's *Learning for Jobs* review of VET in Sweden and Norway, I had interviewed a few apprentices and briefly observed several at work there, in the Netherlands, and in Germany. But I had not seen many apprentices in their natural habitats—their workplaces—and those we were able to question had been prepped for our visit. I needed personal testimony. I wanted to be able to answer skeptics in the United States who challenged, why is it not premature tracking, or simple exploitation, to put sixteen-year-olds to work for more than half the usual school week?

I chose Switzerland for my visits because it was reputed to have among the strongest and most imaginative apprenticeship programs in the world. It is no coincidence that the country is also known for very low youth unemployment, clear pathways from VET to further education, and strong employer engagement. (Youth in many countries were the first group of workers to suffer unemployment increases in the recent downturn, and the average youth unemployment rate in the OECD is now near 20 percent. Switzerland's was just 4.5 percent as of March 2011. In addition, the Swiss have the research, training, and administrative institutions required to support excellence.)

Because in the United States apprenticeships are for training blue-collar workers like plumbers and electricians, and I already had seen my share of automotive shops and student-run restaurants, I focused in Switzerland on what are sometimes called "new apprenticeships." I asked to see and speak with teenagers learning occupations that are key to the global economy, white collar jobs requiring rapidly changing skills in incumbent workers. These professions demand substantial math, writing, and speaking facility, along with the so-called twenty-first-century skills, such as teamwork, solving of messy problems, and intercultural communication. I had read a case of the reform of Swiss commercial training aimed directly at increasing emphasis on these skills. In a six-year process involving 100,000 people that ended with full implementation of the reform in 2003, the Swiss had radically updated what and how young people learned at enterprises like Swisscom and BEKB/BCBE.

Swisscom is the leading telecom provider in the country. In 2010, the company trained 813 apprentices, averaging about 5 percent to 6 percent of 19,500 employees. The Swiss government owns 57 percent of Swisscom, which was founded in 1852 as the national telegraph and postal service. The company went public in 1998 and now serves 5.8 million mobile phone customers and provides around 1.6 million broadband connections. Swisscom's apprentices are chosen from among 7,000 applicants each year. The application review process I witnessed was an initial step in sorting out who would join the company.

BEKB/BCBE is a regional bank with 1,000 employees and a specialty in serving small businesses, those with fewer than 100 employees. BEKB/BCBE trains about 100 apprentices each year, selected from a pool of about 700 applicants. As the bank official responsible for training told me, 10 percent of the company's workplaces are "educational." BEKB/BCBE is strongly oriented toward customer service. Nearly 62 percent of the bank's clients are shareholders, and it has the majority share of personal and small business banking in the Bern area. Established in 1834, with about half of the company now owned by the canton, or state, of Bern, BEKB/BCBE has about $20 million under management. Besides 80 bank sites, it has a mobile bank that visits small towns and villages on a regular weekly schedule, as well as a cyberbank. Extremely proud of the performance of its apprentices on the national exam for commercial training, the bank wants to uphold its record of surpassing the national pass rate—a feat it has accomplished for many years.

On my visit to BEKB/BCBE, I was part of a team including an Australian in charge of youth policy, the heads of the training and IT departments of the bank, several Swiss officials, and the Swiss economics professor who had arranged the visit. We talked with a sixteen-year-old apprentice named Michelle, who was evaluating requests for home improvement loans, and then preparing to phone applicants with a "yes" or "no" and a polite explanation for those denied. She worked with a computer program and confidential electronic applications that gave a detailed picture of each individual's financial status. Three months into her apprenticeship, she was the sole apprentice in an office of about ten regular employees. Later in the year, she would rotate to a different department and learn a different set of competencies on the way to completing her qualifications some three years hence. We asked how she knew what to say to the credit applicants, especially those whose requests she turned down. "They gave me a script," she told us. "But I only needed it at the beginning. Now I know what to say, even when people don't like the answer."

Michelle was one of many young apprentices who appeared mature beyond her age. She told us that she had woken up at 5:30 A.M. in order to take a train, a bus, and a second train to arrive at work by 7:00 A.M., so she could leave early to go shopping with her girlfriends after her eight-hour day. Wearing work-suitable teenage dress—black jeans, a white blouse, and a vest—she readily agreed to lunch with our group of long-time professionals. Totally composed, Michelle told us a bit about why, at fifteen, she had chosen banking as a profession. "When I went to the bank in Thon with my mother, I always liked how people looked," she said. "Everyone dressed so nicely. My father works in the forest, and my brother is an apprentice there. I knew I didn't want to do that." Now just a few short months into her commercial training apprenticeship, she had a different idea about why banking had been a good choice. "I'm going to know a lot about family finances when I'm grown up," she said, "because I am reading all these credit applications, and I see how people have to save money for what they want later." Then she added that she was thinking she would go on to study economics in the university, "once I work here in the bank for a while."

SWITZERLAND'S RETURN ON ITS TRAINING INVESTMENT

Switzerland's apprenticeship system makes for a compelling case study for many reasons, besides the country's low youth unemployment and high employer engagement. Though tiny compared to the United States (the entire country's population is smaller than New York City's), Switzerland's labor market is only slightly more regulated than that of the United States. This is relatively rare among the European Union. Germany and the Nordic countries, for example, have highly regulated labor markets. Swiss success with apprenticeships, then, is not based on the common argument that only countries where it is hard to fire people need apprenticeship systems. That explanation holds that apprenticeships insulate companies against hiring errors, because mistakes are costly, and knowing young people as students and being able to train them to the firm's specifications allows for better hiring decisions. In addition, wages are high and taxes are low in Switzerland. But employers get a return on their educational investments, because the high-quality training prepares the young people to be productive from the start, and their productivity grows each year. With no government subsidies to companies for providing apprenticeship places, trainees know they must earn their keep, and they do.

When I looked into Swiss student achievement, I found that Swiss students are doing well on PISA, the international test of fifteen-year-olds' academic performance. Students scored below the OECD average in reading and science and above in math on the first PISA administration in 2000. The results also showed that socioeconomic background had a significant influence on performance and that variation between lowest and highest performers was large. Surprised and disappointed, the country underwent a wave of education reform with the goal of moving Switzerland up in the rankings.[1] In 2009, Swiss young people—nearly 24 percent of whom are immigrants—had improved. Switzerland is now third internationally in applied math, just behind Finland and Korea, and tenth in science. Reading scores are not as high. But in a culture with many immigrants, four official languages (French, German, Italian, and Romansh), and many children taught in the high German they do not speak at home, Swiss young people might be excused for this lower ranking.

While most Swiss cantons still separate students at the beginning of lower secondary school (around age thirteen) into one of two tracks—schools preparing for a university and those for VET—the country's educational system is increasingly based on choice, not achievement. And VET has considerable status. In a study of the 2000 cohort of Swiss youth, VET was the choice of 42 percent of those who had attained the highest scores (4 and 5) on PISA. In addition, some 19 percent of middle scorers entered the academic track, which leads to a university education, a sign that students chose their pathways based on what interests them most, rather than being placed simply on the basis of grades.[2]

Unlike employers in the Nordic countries, the Netherlands, Austria, and Australia, where the government provides financial incentives for companies to take on apprentices, Swiss employers hire apprentices because this is the most efficient way to screen, prepare, and choose the next generation of workers suited to a particular enterprise. In educating apprentices, their return is higher than if they hired young people right after they finished upper secondary school without work experience and then trained them. The mix of learning in school, at work, and in the training organizations that comprise the Swiss system ensures that employees become productive quickly and efficiently, thereby saving on labor adjustment costs. Finally—and a nuance with considerable importance—while the Germans train some apprentices in virtual or simulated situations located next to, but not in, the "real work," the Swiss put young people directly on the job from the first days of their contract with the company.

HOW SWISSCOM EDUCATES APPRENTICES

Even knowing as I did that the Swiss embraced workplace learning, nothing prepared me for how startling it would be to see so many teenagers actually engaged in learning and work in the commercial and IT sectors of two modern, profitable, mainstream companies. In my mind, sixteen-year-olds resist chores, wear nonconformist clothes, and have precarious relationships with adults. Few have realistic ideas about what type of work they could possibly do in the adult world.

"Isn't it hard for a fifteen-year-old to pick a profession so early?" I asked Alessandro, a charming eighteen-year-old who had finished his apprenticeship and now was working in human resources at Swisscom 60 percent of his time. Italian-speaking at home, German-speaking at school, he was completing English, French, and other academic courses in the other 40 percent of his time. Having once failed the entrance exams for gymnasium (academic upper secondary school), he was now preparing to go on to a university. "When you are fifteen," he said to me in the English he described as "middling" quality, "you want to be an adult, so when you start the job, you feel like an adult. You have income, you are respected, you are more free." I wondered how he decided to apply to Swisscom and asked. "I didn't have any idea what to do," he replied, "but they used a word 'innovative' in their brochure, and I thought that would be interesting."

I had been told that Swisscom's approach to educating its 813 apprentices is not unusual. But to U.S. educator eyes it was extraordinary—the kind of imaginative strategy one might find in the United States in a small, alternative education program, and even there it would be considered cutting edge. My introduction to Swisscom began with its brochure, designed to grab the attention of the fourteen- and fifteen-year-olds the company recruits. On the cover: a picture of a skateboarding boy, hair flying, bent low, sneakers with laces of two different colors, with the headline "Fashion your own future."

Addressing the young reader in the French, German, and Italian familiar "you," the brochure announces that the company educates apprentices in five lines of work: IT specialist or technician, mediamatics technician, telematics technician, commercial employee, and client relations specialist. It then asks interested young people to answer five "yes" or "no" questions:

1. Do you want to be independent and take responsibility for yourself?
2. Do you want to develop freely and shape your own apprenticeship?
3. Do you want to discover your own aptitudes and take initiative?
4. Do you want to take part in team decisions?
5. Do you want to enjoy your work while being productive?

The brochure goes on briefly to describe Swisscom's program: each apprentice has a coach who serves as an advocate and support system as you plan your work; you get to choose from an array of projects to work on, and almost always as part of a team. You keep a journal; you learn to self-assess. And throughout its glossy pages, the French word *autonome* is repeated—meaning you learn to be independent, autonomous, and self-regulating.

At the core of the Swisscom approach is what could be called a Vygotzsky-influenced philosophy. Program designers position young people to stretch beyond their skill levels, but with the scaffolding provided by a coach. The main vehicles for learning are projects lasting from two months to a year. Anyone in the company who has work to be done can post a project on the *qualiportal*, an electronic marketplace organized by job category. Positioned throughout the company are specially trained competency experts who help the apprentices fashion their projects into a set of outcomes related to one of the five fields for which Swisscom trains. The young person, in consultation with the coach, applies to work on a project, undergoes an interview with the team, and usually gets "hired." As the director of human resources, who is responsible for the program, told us, "We don't care if the student knows how to do the job or how long they've been an apprentice, just as long as they are flexible, open, and willing to learn." With the route map of an individualized *qualiplan*, apprentices plan and manage the learning process themselves with the support of their coach.

All apprentices use the numerous tools available on the qualiportal: they search for projects, post their skills profiles, keep a learning journal, track their pathways to assessment, and pass on relevant information to others—all of this, of course, in the three national languages of Switzerland, plus English. At the start of each project, the apprentice defines the targets to be achieved with the worker who posted the job. Thus, an apprentice wanting to learn programming will develop a work plan with his coach for the approval of the employee who will supervise him. He might take on a sophisticated task, teaching himself the requisite skills, as well as relying on the adults around him for expert advice and demonstration. During our visit, we scanned the qualiportal randomly and landed on a job posting from the HR department for an apprentice to join in making a film for employees—a two-month project that looked like a lot of fun.

After the visit to Swisscom's headquarters, we took the train into the main Bern railroad station, where Alessandro and several other HR employees introduced us to apprentices there. In a huge phone store bustling with people, the sixteen-year-old apprentice we interviewed was indistinguishable from the other employees answering questions. His last client, he told us, had a phone that he had diagnosed as having been immersed in water—and thus its problem was not covered under warranty. His challenge was to have the customer go away feeling that she had a reasonable response. Some 250 Swisscom apprentices work all over Switzerland in Swisscom phone stores, visited by their coaches on-site. One store in Bern is maintained entirely by apprentices. "Why would you need three years to train someone to work in a phone store?"

asked the skeptical Australian government official who had come along on our visit. "You could learn how to sell phones in two or three months."

But this was the wrong frame for the question. Of course, one could learn to sell phones in three months, or even less, but the phone store apprenticeship filled quite a different need in the development of the sixteen- to eighteen-year-olds who chose this route to the "working life." Likely not the most ambitious of young people, the phone store apprentices were participating in a three-year structured transition to adulthood. They were paid and were productive; they participated on an intergenerational team; they did real work that was consequential to Swisscom and enough traditional schoolwork each week to hone their academic knowledge. With their coaches' help, they would be able to choose among a variety of options as the years went on. Perhaps some of them, like Alessandro and Michelle, would end up headed for a university. Others, like the young man we interviewed who was teaching himself in depth about the latest phone technology, would be on the road to a supervisory role in a phone store. It would be unlikely, however, that these young people would drop out of school, lack for ideas about the future, or arrive at the age of majority without understanding their own interests, skills, and competencies.

OTHER APPRENTICESHIPS IN OTHER COUNTRIES

While I've seen nothing as educationally radical as Swisscom's apprenticeship program in Norway, Sweden, the Netherlands, or Germany, the more ordinary apprentice role is interesting, too. It also is easier to think of replicating in small companies. Take Norway, with its two-plus-two system (two years of schooling and two years of apprenticeship) and its commitment to finding workplaces that meet the needs of every young person—including those in isolated rural areas where transportation between villages may be possible only by boat and hardly at all in the winter. Up above the Arctic Circle near Bodo, in 2009, my *Learning for Jobs* team visited a training site for young people in the village of Inndyr who wanted to enter Norway's fish farming industry, as well as a solar wafer factory in Glomfjord, a few hundred kilometers down the coast. The very personal, individualized character of much of apprenticeship training was evident in both sites.

In the tiny school in Inndyr, with its view out onto the waters of the fjord that houses the fisheries, four apprentices met with us, along with their teachers. To the question, why did you choose fish farming, came the answer from one student, "I love the smell of the sea," and from a second, the only girl, "I really love horses, so I'm doing fish farming four days, and then for Fridays, the school found me a place to work with a veterinarian who takes care of horses." One teacher sat nearby, a PhD conducting research on aquaculture. The school doubles as a state research facility, and the students explained their instructor's research on the health of farmed salmon, as he sat listening attentively. At lunch, the twelve- and thirteen-year-olds who maintain a moneymaking restaurant in their school (entrepreneurs as young as eight or nine run small businesses in many Norwegian schools) appeared in their chefs' hats and aprons to serve their specialty, a delicious fish soup.

In Glomsfjord, the apprentice trainer, a thirtysomething in jeans, told us how he often rode his bike around town in the mornings to make sure his students were awake, dressed, and prepared to be at work on time. Many young people in rural Norway leave home at age fifteen or sixteen to attend vocational school and become apprentices. They live with host families or on their own with other students, so often the apprentice trainer plays a parental role along with that of coach and teacher.

In Oslo, I saw typical, but contrasting urban apprentices: one group at work at Cathinka Guldberg-senteret, a 125-bed nursing home on the campus of a hospital; another at Norway's largest international media, publishing, and design company, the 07 Group. These two apprentices—Adelina, a teenage Macedonian immigrant learning to care for geriatric patients, and Linn, a sophisticated graphic designer in her early twenties—came to their apprenticeships from very different circumstances. As the lively director of professional development who supervised the nursing home apprentices told me, "No one wants to do this work, so we have to recruit, and we often get young people with problems of their own and not the highest school grades, or young people who don't speak Norwegian well." Adelina, the young Macedonian woman, was in this field for two reasons: she was just mastering Norwegian, and she wanted to go to nursing school so she could join the profession of her aunt and sister. The graphic design slot was extremely competitive—applicants needed portfolios, experience, and excellent grades, and were interviewed. Linn already had a university bachelor's degree in visual communication and had sought the position in the 07 Group because she believed this work placement would increase her value in the labor market.

What stood out for me, however, had little to do with these two young women, as bright and enthusiastic as they were, but with the adult professionals introducing them. To put it simply, both showed pleasure, pride, and a deep sense of responsibility for the young people in their charge. Olaug Vibe, the director of professional development at the nursing home, had written to me when I asked to visit: "We have seven apprentices by now. Learning to work is so helpful to them, and I find it very motivating and fun to work with these young ones!" Meeting her with her young student, she carefully helped Adelina tell me about the many responsibilities she had. Among the things she was learning to do: checking the care plans of her two patients every morning; bathing one, an elderly man who needed substantial help; caring for another through his death; and managing her sorrow when her patient died—the hardest part.

Havard Grjotheim, the president of the 07 Group, who had welcomed me to the company, sat in on my talk with Linn. He had his own view of apprenticeship and why such an investment is good for a company, first sounding the same theme as Olaug Vibe. "By having apprentices, our company gets into close contact with the new generation, their way of acting and thinking," he said. "This is great for our organization—for the environment, for the culture of the company." He added the classic rationale: "Later on, we can hire these young people who know our company well from their apprenticeship period, and that also creates loyalty to our company and our customers." Then he paused, and added a few words that signal not just appreciation for the younger generation, but responsibility for them, too: "Each one of these young people is someone's son or daughter," he said.

5

Changing the Outcomes
of Youth Left Behind

Policies and Practices That Protect and Support

All OECD countries have a group of youth left behind. These are the dropouts who do not complete upper secondary school or those staying marginally connected to school but unlikely to achieve the outcomes required for a diploma, qualification, or apprenticeship contract. These young people are often members of immigrant or minority groups, live in underresourced rural areas, are members of families with low educational attainment, or have personal, financial, and family problems that distract them from school. This is the group on whom the current financial crisis is having a devastating impact. According to a recent report from the OECD's *Jobs for Youth* review, by the middle of 2010, the number of young people aged fifteen to twenty-four who were neither in education nor in employment or training (the group often called "NEET") had risen from 10.8 percent of the age group in 2008 to 12.5 percent. This represents 16.7 million youth. Among them, many are already far removed from the labor market, because they either have been unemployed for more than a year or were inactive and did not seek a job.[1]

In the United States today, high school dropouts with low skills are receiving considerable attention, if not effective programming. This is a large group in numbers because of the sheer size of the U.S. population, and because the youth cohort size is declining at a slower rate in the United States than in most European countries. The risk is that during the current recession, this group will account for a good deal of the rising unemployment rate and will grow larger as more youth experience longer periods of unemployment after leaving education.

Multiple research studies confirm that for young people, especially those with lower levels of education, long-term unemployment that occurs early and continues for lengthy periods takes a heavy toll, can diminish their earnings over a lifetime, and "scar" the job seeker permanently.[2] Not only do such young people have a longer time than adults to suffer the consequences of joblessness, they are at a formative stage of development; thus their behavior and attitudes in relation to work may be permanently molded by the experience.[3] Unemployment thwarts dreams and curtails ambition.

The U.S. teen (ages sixteen to nineteen) employment rate of 45.2 percent in 2000 fell to 28.6 percent in June 2010. And hardest hit are low-income teens of color, the very group who struggle in underperforming schools, and who most need the income and structure that jobs provide. In this prosperous country, it seems a cruel irony that the employment rate of upper-middle-class teens (with family incomes of $75,000 to $100,000) is 41 percent, four times higher than the rate for low-income African American teens.

The effectiveness of an education system might be judged not by how well it does with top and middle performers, but by how it manages to educate those least equipped to succeed. That is, one might put countries and their education systems to the test by asking tough questions about their struggling young people: how many are there, how do the education and social service systems serve them, what policies address their needs and hopes, and what are the results? Unfortunately, by this measure, the United States is not doing well either in keeping high percentages of young people engaged in school and preparing for a career or in supporting their transition into productive work. With urban high school noncompletion rates of 50 percent, the TV and newspaper headlines are justified in calling dropout a crisis, a silent epidemic, or an emergency, and in publicizing the frightening figures: 7,200 students drop out of U.S. schools every day, adding up to 1.3 million a year. This chapter asks what successful education systems do to improve the chances of young people struggling to gain a foothold

146

in the labor market leading to productive adulthood. Below I take a close look at several countries with higher upper secondary completion rates, lower youth unemployment, and a reasonably rapid transition of young people into the job market after completing schooling, and ask how these "higher completion" countries deal with low achievers. But first this section explores some commonalities in the policies and practices of more successful countries.

WHAT CONSTITUTES "SUCCESS" FOR YOUNG PEOPLE LEFT BEHIND?

Caution is required in comparing U.S. high schools with upper secondary schools. In many OECD countries, compulsory school ends at around age fourteen or fifteen; upper secondary schools are separate institutions serving sixteen- to nineteen-year-olds. While U.S. high schools and upper secondary schools share the same International Standard Classification of Education (ISCED) classification (Level 3), vocational program completers outside of the United States have attained work credentials and experience closer to that of a career-focused associate's degree than a high school diploma. Thus recapturing dropouts or retaining students at risk and keeping them in school through completion can be counted as a success in that the student has a credential more useful in the marketplace than most high school diplomas in the United States.

Since a purpose of education about which everyone agrees is preparation for a vocation or career, a second way to define success is to ask which countries have kept the highest percentages of young people in school and transitioned them most successfully from schooling to work. What percentage of youth are employed? Some countries are doing substantially better than others by their young people.[4] Here is the critical data since the economic crisis: from a youth unemployment rate in 2008 of about 11 percent—3 to 5 points lower than the OECD average (14.4 percent)—by September 2010, the U.S. rate had risen, along with the OECD average, to above 18 percent and is continuing to rise. In the same crisis, youth in the countries profiled here—Australia, Austria, Germany, the Netherlands, Norway, and Switzerland—were in the 5 to 8 percent range in September 2010, with lower rates to begin with and smaller-than-average increases.[5] (See as well, figure I.1 in the introduction.)

Some general patterns emerge: countries with strong vocational programs in which large percentages of students participate have high attainment, completion, and youth employment rates. We can hypothesize that the VET system may serve to retain students who might not have stayed in school if the only option were academic and fully classroom based. VET students also have risk factors that can predict dropout. The majority are from middle to lower socioeconomic backgrounds, have less-well-educated parents, and score less well on PISA, the international assessment of student achievement, than students in the academic track. Beyond this data, some other patterns emerge. VET students complete programs leading to a university at lower rates than students in general. Among VET systems, however, those that require students to chose between vocational and academic programs earliest (Germany, Switzerland, the Netherlands) have higher completion rates than those in which students are in comprehensive programs through age fifteen or sixteen.

"At Risk" Young People in VET

Young people vulnerable to failure fall into two groups whose predicaments overlap: those who drop out of vocational education before completing upper secondary school, and those who are low performers in the VET system—young people who may complete school, but not attain a final qualification or simply have grades too low for any company to want to contract with them for an apprenticeship or hire them for a permanent job. The latter group presents a special challenge to VET systems; unlike dropouts, these young people have a public record of low achievement although they have met some minimal level of education. Indeed, in the current tight job market, VET systems face problems in maintaining sufficient apprenticeship places to serve all the well-qualified students whether places are government subsidized or not, and so these low achievers are particularly at risk. A number of the effective strategies outlined here evolve from their governments' policy perspective: that young people do better in combinations of work and learning, so if a standard apprenticeship place is not available, school authorities must compensate by providing an equivalent experience.

Interestingly, some of the stronger VET systems do not have much success in getting low-achieving or disengaged students the skills they need to enter the job market. That is, for all their success with the majority of young people, they are still trying to figure out how to educate and integrate the remaining 5 to 10 percent of young people into the mainstream labor force. For example, Germany has an upper secondary completion rate of over 90 percent, but also has a group of migrant and ethnic minority students who do not get a foothold in the job market. In Germany, one negative consequence of early tracking is that the young people in the least competitive track (*Hauptschule*) leave school with weaker academic skills and consequently have a difficult time finding an apprenticeship. For such students, Germany has established a number and variety of "transition" programs, on which it spends a great deal of money to produce relatively modest results. Approximately 15 percent of German young people opting for the VET pathway fail to obtain a labor market qualification by their mid-twenties. Among young people who are labeled "migrants"—some of whom may in fact be children or grandchildren of people born in Germany—the numbers are much worse (36 percent without qualification).

Most countries with VET systems that serve the majority have attacked the dropout problem creatively and systematically with effective policies and practices that mix school and work. Countries such as Australia and Norway have a relatively larger group than Austria, Switzerland, the Netherlands, or Germany that the mainstream VET system does not serve successfully; and if these young people are ignored, their plight is visible and can become a controversial policy problem, because social services for them are costly.

Policies and Practices That Keep Young People Learning

While countries' analyses of why students drop out are remarkably similar—boredom, language difficulties, failing grades, lack of relevance, personal and financial problems—there are differences among countries in solutions. The countries of interest are Australia, Austria, the Netherlands, Norway, and Switzerland. Each of these countries is concerned about the social and monetary costs of dropout, as well as about equity of outcomes and social inclusion of their newer and growing immigrant populations and other struggling young people.[6]

What policies and practices stand out in the countries that do the best with young people in danger of being left behind either in school completion or in access to apprenticeships, traineeships, and jobs? First, these countries have a mainstream alternative to university preparation—vocational education—that can be adapted to serve struggling young people, although its main purpose is to launch the majority of young people into careers. The links to the labor market are built into the system, and employers can be incentivized to work with harder-to-integrate young people, just as young people can be pushed in various ways to enter an education program. For dropouts, it would appear to be a more appealing prospect to be recruited back into an education system in which one learns while working than one that requires sitting in a classroom all day.

Second, these countries send strong signals to youth, their families, and communities through youth policies—sometimes coercive ones—that it is not all right to enter adulthood without completing at least upper secondary vocational education. To underscore this point, a number of countries are now requiring young people to stay in school or in a work and learning program until the age of eighteen. The more successful countries make explicit commitments enforced in legislation to protect and support young people as a special population group. The best polices are both universal and targeted. That is, legislation defines the rights and responsibilities for all young people, but the government also takes it as its responsibility to ensure through its social security systems that the most vulnerable actually attain what is promised. Such youth policies act to prevent *social exclusion*, a recurrent term in government statements about dropout prevention that refers to discrimination or bearing a stigma of some sort.[7] The first two categories below are youth policy options; the third and fourth are commonly used practices:

- *Youth guarantees.* The notion of youth guarantees of schooling, training, and jobs is gaining popularity as governments struggle to protect young people from the economic downturn. Australia, Austria, the United Kingdom, Norway, the Netherlands, and New Zealand have such policies. The European Union is working to create a youth guarantee that will ensure young people under the age of twenty-five who have left the labor market or school the entitlement to a job, apprenticeship, or other education within six months. From 2010 on, this entitlement will be provided after four months and includes income supports.[8]

- *Mutual obligation policies.* Called "activation policies," these entail agreements or compacts among young people, their families, and the government that the young person will actively seek work and stay in training in exchange for targeted actions to help them. Income supports and other services are in jeopardy if the young person refuses services or does not keep her side of the bargain in participation.

- *Adapted work and learning programs.* The VET pathway is altered or adapted to serve at-risk youth: programs can be shorter, have a balance more toward application than theory, and include social supports. Generally, financial incentives are available to employers, or schools construct simulated work situations to parallel a full apprenticeship.

- *Intensive career guidance and counseling.* Although this is among the weakest areas in even good VET systems, some countries *do* have effective career education (learning about the world of work) and individual career advising—sometimes mandatory—which can be coupled with psychological counseling. In addition, bridge- or transition-year courses are an option for students uncertain about their interests and the right pathway choice, and who wish to try out several possible occupations. (See examples in figure 5.1 of career exploration strategies in Norway and the Germanic countries.)

Some countries and the European Union have taken steps to strengthen and expand these approaches in the last year to protect the most vulnerable youth from the impact of the fiscal crisis. Figure 5.2

FIGURE 5.1   Work experience

In Norway, nearly all students in lower secondary education, regardless of whether they are or are not intending to enter a VET program, have one week of work experience in their ninth grade and some further work placement in grade 10. Schools often establish partnerships with local companies to facilitate exchanges between students and employers. Most lower-secondary students in Denmark also have an opportunity to get a flavor of a real work environment. Between the ages of 14 and 16 they usually undertake at least two different one-week work placements.[a]

In Germany, Switzerland, and Austria students in lower secondary programs leading to apprenticeships have short work placements in companies. Their purpose is to provide young people with firsthand work experience which would help them to choose their career path and to find an apprenticeship place. Often these short work placements take place during the school holidays but students can also be given free time during the school year to attend them. A survey of around 1,000 secondary school students in Switzerland showed that these short work placements are a most important source of information for their professional career choice. 61% of these young people were offered an apprenticeship place upon completion of the workplace experience.[b]

[a,b]OECD, *OECD Review of Career Guidance Policies: Country Note Norway*, (Paris: OECD Publishing, 2002), www.oecd.org/dataoecd/38/24/1937973.pdf

Source: Recreated from OECD, *Learning for Jobs: OECD Reviews of Vocational Education and Training* (Paris: OECD Publishing, 2010), box 3.4, http://dx.doi. org/10.1787/9789264087460-en. Used with permission.

includes recommendations from the *Jobs for Youth* review for France, where youth unemployment is of crisis proportions.

Australia

With a bifurcated attainment pattern—high rates of postsecondary completion and high rates of dropout from upper secondary school—Australia is struggling to improve the chances for youth left behind, a large proportion of whom are aboriginal peoples living in impoverished and isolated rural areas. Australia has a robust youth labor market, with 47 percent of fifteen- to nineteen-year-olds holding some kind of job, and a relatively low youth unemployment rate. Young people act on the substantial temptation to leave school for low-wage jobs. In April 2010, the liberal government released a new youth strategy

FIGURE 5.2   From an emergency plan to a strategy "Acting for Youth" in France

The emergency plan for youth employment launched in April 2009 in France aims to:

1. Facilitate the school-to-work transition by promoting apprenticeship and combined work and training opportunities. Any company that recruits a young apprentice before [the end of] June 2010 will be exempt from paying social security charges for that person for a period of one year. Furthermore, small enterprises (with fewer than 50 employees) will receive an additional, direct subsidy of EUR 1,800. The government will also finance 170,000 new *contrats de professionnalisation* by mid-2010, up from 145,000 in 2008. Under this type of contract, work experience is alternated with formal training. As an incentive for companies to offer these contracts, the plan proposes a direct one-off subsidy, worth EUR 1,000 for each person aged less than 26 who signs up. If the person has not achieved an educational qualification equivalent to the *baccalauréat* school certificate (academic or vocational), the subsidy is doubled to EUR 2,000.

2. Promote the transformation of internships into permanent employment contracts (*contrats à durée indéterminée*, or CDIs). Firms who made this change before the end of September 2009 will receive a payment from the state of EUR 3,000 per head.

3. Provide additional training and employment opportunities for youth far removed from the labor market. The government will finance jointly with the PES 50,000 training programs for unskilled youth to help them gain a qualification and will subsidize 50,000 additional hirings in the private sector and 30,000 additional contracts in the public sector, both targeted towards disadvantaged youth. The latter measure refers to the creation of *emplois passerelles*. These subsidized contracts in the public sector at the local level are geared to the acquisition of transferrable skills that can be put in good use in the private sector (e.g., computing skills, childcare, and property management).

In September 2009, these employment measures were reinforced in the broader youth strategy "Acting for youth" dealing also with: improving guidance in school; preventing 17–18-year-olds from dropping out of school; helping youth to become financially autonomous; and encouraging youth to become better citizens.

Source: Recreated from S. Scarpetta, A. Sonnet, and T. Manfredi, "Rising Youth Unemployment During The Crisis: How to Prevent Negative Long-term Consequences on a Generation?," OECD Social, Employment and Migration Working Papers, no. 106 (Paris: OECD Publishing, 2010), http://dx.doi.org/10.1787/5kmh79zb2mmv-en. Used with permission.

developed by the Council of Australian Governments (COAG) entitled Compact with Young Australians. The policy implements education and training requirements for fifteen- to twenty-four-year-olds who have left or are thinking of leaving school without completing upper secondary education, "providing protection from the anticipated tighter labor market, and ensuring they would have the qualifications needed to take up the jobs as the economy recovered":

> [The compact] has three elements to promote skills acquisition and ensure young people are learning or earning," which exemplify a "mutual obligation" policy. The elements include:
>
> - A National Youth Participation Requirement which requires all young people to participate in schooling (or an approved equivalent) to Year 10, and then participate full-time (at least 25 hours per week) in education, training or employment, or a combination of these activities, until age 17.
> - An entitlement to an education or training place for low-income 15 to 24 year olds which focuses on attaining Year 12 or equivalent qualifications . . . Entitlement places are for government-subsidized qualifications, subject to admission requirements and course availability. (For 20-24 year olds who already have a Year 12 or equivalent qualification, the entitlement is to a place that would result in them attaining a higher qualification than they currently hold.)
> - Participation requirements for those under the age of 21 to be eligible for income support through Youth Allowance or the Family Tax Benefit include participation in education and training full-time, or in part-time study or training in combination with other approved activities, usually for at least 25 hours per week, until they attain Year 12 or an equivalent Certificate Level II qualification. Young people not participating in their Employment Pathway Plan may lose their Youth Allowance.[9]

Beginning in January 2010, the government awarded contracts to registered training organizations (RTOs) for intensive services under the banner of the Australian Apprenticeships Access Program. This service is designed to provide vulnerable youth who experience barriers to entering skilled employment with nationally recognized prevocational training, support, and assistance, in preparation for an Australian apprenticeship. The program includes a minimum of 150 hours of nationally recognized, accredited prevocational training linked to an Australian apprenticeship pathway. Following the training period, participants receive individualized intensive job search assistance for up to thirteen weeks. Participants who gain an apprenticeship or other employment or enter further education or training, along with their employers, receive thirteen weeks of postplacement support.[10]

Austria

With 80 percent of students opting for VET after completing lower secondary school, the Austrian VET system is the mainstream system of schooling.[11] Within VET, about 40 percent select the dual system, which can be preceded by a prevocational year; about 15 percent attend school-based VET; and another 27 percent enroll in a VET college, where after five years they can acquire a double qualification: a VET diploma and the requirements to enter a university. This last option has been in place since 2008 and is increasingly popular. VET also takes place at the tertiary level in the universities of applied sciences (*Fachhochschulen*), in postsecondary VET colleges (*Akademien*), and in the form of postsecondary VET courses.

An apprenticeship can take between two and four years, but most last for three years. Approximately 75 percent of the time is spent in a training firm, the remaining 25 percent in a part-time VET school. (This can vary across trades.) Apprentices sign a contract and earn a salary that increases each year, reaching roughly 80 percent of a starting wage in the final year. Salaries are determined in collective bargaining.

"Young people" are the group of persons supported most intensively under current labor market policies—signaling the society's commitment to the future of the next generation. Austria has among the lowest youth unemployment rates in the EU, and aggressive policies and programs to ensure that all young people have support to complete a qualification and enter the workforce. The government has ramped up its youth policy since the beginning of the financial crisis in 2009 to ensure that young people needing special support to transition from school to work receive help.

Because so many young people enter working life through the dual system, Austria faces a shortage of apprenticeship places (see figure 5.3), despite the fact that the Austrian government, unlike the German or Swiss governments, subsidizes companies providing training slots. The youth guarantee takes the form of either a subsidized apprenticeship place, an alternative training program, or a subsidized occupational activity. Run by the Public Employment Service, these targeted programs served roughly 60 percent of the young people registered as apprenticeship seekers or unemployed. In concrete terms, this means that six out of ten persons aged fifteen to twenty-four registered as unemployed or as seeking apprenticeship places received support.

Not surprising, students who are low performers, immigrants or migrants, or socially disadvantaged or disabled in some way are those that have difficulty finding apprenticeship slots. To decrease dropout rates, the government has intensified vocational training and vocational counseling starting in 7th grade and has strengthened links between educational institutions and regional training providers. Among the more interesting of the Austrian interventions are programs for socially disadvantaged or academically weak students who take part

FIGURE 5.3 Apprenticeship places and apprenticeship seekers

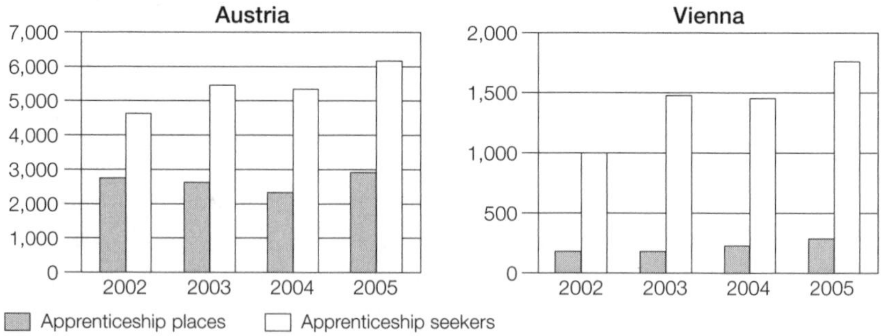

Source: Adapted from Kathrin Hoeckel, *Learning for Jobs: OECD Reviews of Vocational Education and Training*, Austria (Paris: OECD Publishing, 2010), fig. 2.1, box 2.5, www .oecd.org/edu/learningforjobs. Used with permission.

in integrative vocational training (UBA courses), which allows them to extend the normal training period or to complete only parts of the training but still receive a professional diploma.

Based on §30 of the Vocational Training Act, ÜBA courses (*Überbetriebliche Ausbildung*) are now legally recognized as equivalent to regular apprenticeships, and ÜBA apprentices also pursue the final assessment of an apprenticeship. Although these courses were initially designed to lead young people into regular apprenticeships after one year, more and more young people stay in ÜBA centers for the entire period of training. These programs do not have all the strengths of the "regular" dual system—especially those where companies are simulated (see figure 5.4). Nonetheless, with such robust labor market outcomes for young people, it appears that this rather expensive Austrian intervention is a useful investment.

Along with the options above, the Austrians are establishing *Production Schools* to facilitate the transition from school to vocational training or to work for young people with major problems or special support requirements—in particular, those dropping out from apprenticeships or school. These schools are designed for young people "tired of school;" the programs combine workshops, creative methods, and

FIGURE 5.4 Überbetriebliche Ausbildung (ÜBA)

ÜBA courses are delivered in two modalities. Modality 1 aims to provide a full program in ÜBA centers and does not aim to find regular training places in companies for students. The Austrian Labour Market Service aims to offer this modality to half of the students who cannot find a regular apprenticeship, and train the remaining half under modality 2.

Under modality 2, most of the training is provided in simulated companies (*Praxisbetriebe*). In addition, students receive sociopedagogical support from ÜBA centers and help to find a regular apprenticeship place. Under this modality, the training contract is for a maximum of one year, as the key objective is to encourage students to migrate to regular apprenticeship places. About half of the students shift to a regular apprenticeship in the first year of training. Those who do not manage to find a regular apprenticeship can complete their training in the simulated companies.

Source: Adapted from Kathrin Hoeckel and Robert Schwartz, *Learning for Jobs: OECD Reviews of Vocational Education and Training*, Germany (Paris: OECD Publishing, 2010), box 2.8, www.oecd.org/edu/learningforjobs. Used with permission.

ongoing support by social workers. As described by the Federal Ministry of Labor, Social Affairs and Consumer Protection:

> The Production Schools do not offer complete training programs but allow young people to gain practical experience in workshops, which helps them in choosing a future apprenticeship or job. The outcome is therefore very individual; a participant may for example decide to continue attending the school from which he/she had dropped out, or a young person may have discovered his/her interest in a specific occupation through practical work and enter an apprenticeship in a company. Production Schools offer a wide range of occupations—from media design and creative textile production to wood processing. The young people obtain a basic qualification in a training phase lasting up to nine months and are supported in personal development.[12]

The Netherlands

The percentage of young people aged eighteen to twenty-four who do not have an upper secondary qualification was 15.5 percent in 2001. The country set a goal in 2002 to cut early school leaving in half by 2011—from 70,000 each year to 35,000 in the 2010-2011 school year. In 2009-2010, the most recent year for which data is available, the number had been reduced to 39,600, almost at the target. The government's new target for 2012 is that there be no more than 35,000 drop outs.[13] To achieve this success, the Dutch have mounted an aggressive, multipronged "blitz" on dropouts. In 2005, the Dutch government passed the Youth Care Act, a youth strategy focused on at-risk young people, with the goal of bringing coherence to services and making them more effective. In parallel, a Youth Unemployment Task Force adopted three strategies for reducing youth unemployment (which is already among the lowest rates in Europe):

- Ensure that young people obtain a basic qualification, and prevent early leaving.

- Pursue an active approach to structural youth unemployment, combined with compulsory working and learning programs.

• Conduct an intensive supervision and development program, as well as a system for tracking every student's school participation on a daily basis.

Currently, the Ministry of Education, Culture and Science is responsible for guiding and coordinating youth policy across the ministries of Health, Welfare and Sports; Social Affairs and Employment; and Justice.[14]

As of fall 2008, young people who had not obtained an upper secondary diploma by age eighteen were required to be in a full-time or part-time education program, had to have a job, or a combination of both. Those aged eighteen to twenty-seven who had not completed an upper secondary qualification were required to enroll in a mandatory work/study activity (*Leerwerkplicht Wet, Kwalificatieplicht Wet*). Students can chose among four options to obtain the qualification—programs of one, two, three, or four years (with the longest program leading to universities of applied sciences). If they reject such an offer, they can be subject to loss of income support.

Such "activation" or "mutual obligation" policies may seem punitive to Americans in that the young person can be denied income support. But in countries that provide generous social and educational support to individuals, as in the Netherlands and the Nordic countries, such policies have a different resonance because they exist as part of a broader social contract. Dutch educators with whom we spoke believe that it is responsible policy to require young people to have the minimum qualification to enter the labor market.

The Netherlands has both universal and targeted social and financial supports. All Dutch families receive a child support allowance for children up to age eighteen; this monthly payment can go for books and school expenses not paid for by government means-tested scholarships and loans. Those over eighteen receive monthly support directly, with a larger amount for those not living at home. In addition, the Netherlands has long had a school finance system that targets additional per-pupil funding to schools taking students with disadvantages.

A combination of incentives, rewards, and programmatic initiatives are keeping an impressive number of young people in school through the completion of a qualification. First, all students are tracked by a unique Education Number linked to demographic, employment, and benefit information, and sufficiently detailed to track dropouts by neighborhood. Second, a Digital Absence Portal records standardized attendance data across the country daily. Third, through the Kafka Brigade, an applied research method, the government engages young people in describing the barriers and problems they encounter in getting help from the system. As a result, policy is now developed starting with the student, rather than with the system or institutions.[15]

As a result of Kafka inquiry, the government took steps to reduce student encounters with the bureaucracy by assigning a single case manager to each student. In addition, schools are being held accountable for the outcomes with at-risk young people. With dropout reduction numerical goals set forth in regional convenants, schools must develop their own strategies to ensure that truants are made responsible, that student problems are identified and addressed, that students are introduced to careers and have post compulsory school programs of study or work. Schools receive 2,500 euros for each single reduction in dropout from the previous year, for a total of 250 million euros for the country. The local authorities serve as partners to schools, enforcing the Compulsory Education Act, and seeing that Drop-out Registration and Coordination Centers provide appropriate services and cooperate with Debt Assistance and Addiction Care providers. In response to the Kafka data indicating that young people want and need more work-based options and better counseling, the government has established a system to accredit prior learning of eighteen- to twenty-three-year-olds, and has engaged large employers in helping twenty thousand young people gain basic qualifications. The government has also engaged the centers of expertise—the seventeen intermediary organizations that link the labor market, employers, and schools to place upper secondary students in work sites—in keeping with the Youth Unemployment Action Plan.

Norway
Under a system in Norway introduced in 1995 and revised in 2009 by the coalition government, all youth below the age of twenty-five have a right to three years of free upper secondary education to be completed

before the age of twenty-four within a five-year period. Youth who are unemployed and not enrolled in education have a right to a job or to participate in employment programs. The guarantee is not a legal right, but is advanced as a promise to youth. To ensure that the guarantee is operational, all counties are required to track and provide individualized counseling for youth between the ages of sixteen and twenty-one who are outside of education and employment (*Oppfølgingstjenesten*). The county must provide an individual program for each youth and coordinate the development of his or her pathway with other social service agencies. Given its extraordinary wealth, Norway can afford such personalized services, which are especially important because many young people live in isolated rural communities where, outside of school or an apprenticeship position, it is challenging to find alternative options.[16]

Norway researchers, policy makers, and educators express continuing concern about the substantial dropout rate from initial vocational education. While Norway has high completion rates in general—over 90 percent—students take a long time to finish their schooling. VET students both graduate at lower rates than students in the university track and take longer times to complete. Looking at the 2002 cohort, Norwegian researchers note that while "95 percent of students graduating from compulsory education in the spring term 2002 enrolled in upper secondary education the same year, only 66 percent had completed upper secondary education 5 years later." While about 55 percent of students chose a VET pathway, only about 50 percent of these have successfully completed their studies and apprenticeship and have gained a qualification.[17]

Norway has struggled to address its dropout problem. While the Norwegian economy is thriving, and this very rich country has an unemployment rate of 3.6 percent, and young people without credentials do get jobs, Norwegians know that the future is not secure for non-credentialed young people. There are particular equity concerns also since dropouts and those with difficulty getting apprenticeships include disproportionate percentages of darker-skinned young men from non-Western countries.

For students struggling with school, Norway in 2007 piloted and has continued a shorter upper secondary VET program—two years of integrated work and learning rather than two years of school followed by one to two years of apprenticeship. One impulse for creating this alternative is Norwegian research showing that "prolongation of the VET tracks and the increase of academic content led to an increase in the probability of dropout among the low performing students, although the overall achievement level increased among the VET students."[18] The certificate of practice leads to a lower-level degree recognized by industry, rather than the full four-year VET upper secondary diploma, but it is not a dead end. Once they have their certificate, students may complete their full upper secondary degree by adding on the remaining two years.

While Norwegians and the OECD *Learning for Jobs* team had some reservations about creating a track that could exacerbate inequities, the research-based evaluation of the pilot has so far yielded positive results that suggest that these worries are not warranted. Students, teachers, and trainers are mostly favorable to the measure, and the dropout rates are thus far very low. In addition, and unanticipated, 65 percent of the students gained the motivation to continue their education and training in order to earn the full upper secondary certificate. Considering that VET students in Norway have dropout or "transfer out" rates close to 45 percent, the implementation of such a policy measure could lead to some substantial improvement.[19]

It is also important to note that the new program follows the most progressive structure for VET: learning is contextualized, and disciplines are embedded or integrated into application. As noted in chapter 4, Oslo is building a school to promulgate such an integrated model for a range of students, and the pilot has provided an opportunity to try the idea out.

Switzerland

Switzerland should get the award for the VET system having it all or almost all. The Swiss manage to educate a very high proportion of their young people successfully in the apprenticeship system and transition them successfully into employment. The youth unemployment rate is below 5 percent in 2011. The Swiss government's goal is to reduce the number of young people who do not attain an upper secondary qualification from 10 percent to 5 percent by 2015. Some key strengths of the Swiss system include imaginative approaches to teaching and learning in companies; required and high-quality education for VET teachers and company trainers; a collaborative and reliable method for developing and revising career training programs (competencies, assessments, curriculum, etc.); strong participation from social partners in providing apprenticeships without government subsidy; and a clear set of standards for high-quality employer-run training.

Given these strengths, it is not surprising that a recent study of the level of well-being among adolescents in Switzerland notes that "social competences such as compassion, acceptance of responsibility and willingness to achieve are very well developed among young people."[20] The Swiss manage to accomplish this in a federal system with no minister of education and strong cantonal power. They do, however, have extensive federal agencies that provide support to the VET system, carry out research and training, and monitor results at the national and cantonal levels.

Nonetheless, the Swiss do have challenges. About one-third of the Swiss population is under thirty, and about 25 percent of this group are immigrants to Switzerland. These are the young people of greatest concern. Late arrivals to Switzerland may not be well integrated into school or may have low achievement levels. According to the Federal Migration Office, "between 15 and 20% of an age cohort of foreign youngsters do not go through regular vocational training and thus have a higher risk of unemployment and dependence on social welfare benefits." Immigrant students who enter VET also have a harder time finding an apprenticeship.[21]

A number of mechanisms are in place to prevent dropout, and to support the transition to and through an appropriate VET program. Among these, two especially noteworthy interventions are the *bridge year*, a form of preapprenticeship, available after lower secondary school for students who are unsure about next steps; and *case management*, a system in place to identify and support individual students at risk. Bridge-year programs are available after year 9 of compulsory school and are intended for students who have not performed well, for those who have not yet found an apprenticeship, or for those who have not decided on an occupational area. The course includes practical training and preapprenticeship. Bridge-year courses prepare students for admission to upper secondary–level VET programs. Once enrolled, students are rarely dismissed from either the school-based or the work-based component without a long period of warning and counseling; vocational teachers and vocational trainers are in constant contact about the behavior and success of apprentices, so that they share information and corrective strategies about students who are not doing well. The Swiss education system is particularly focused on making such options available in the event that the fiscal crisis, from which Switzerland has been quite protected, diminishes the number of apprentice places available, leaving the least well-prepared students adrift.[22]

Case management is a new strategy intended to provide intensive support to the 2 percent to 3 percent of young people whose entry into working life is severely jeopardized. The target group includes socially excluded young people, those with personal or family difficulties, or those with weak academic skills. The confederation provides additional financial support to the cantons to intervene to prevent school dropout or unemployment, rather than wait until problems are severe. Case managers identify at-risk students in the second year of lower secondary, and stay with them to and through the completion of a VET program.[23]

Finally, the Swiss have one of the strongest systems of career guidance and counseling to advise and support students at key transition points in their education and career development. The services exemplify an approach that is both universal and targeted to those needing special advice and support. Attending career guidance and information sessions is mandatory for students in compulsory secondary education. In years 7, 8, and 9 of lower secondary school, students learn in their own schools about their career options and are introduced to the main institutions for guidance and counseling: centers for occupational information (*Berufsinformationszentren*, or *BIZ*). These freestanding centers provide information and counseling for all levels of VET at a neutral site away from the schools. Here young people can see generalist counselors and specialists in specific fields. Counselors receive training to ensure that they are well informed about VET courses and the labor markets, rather than the more usual training in psychology.

CONCLUSION

While the dropout crisis in the United States is deeply troubling, it is not as if there aren't creative people effectively at work to keep young people engaged in school. But what contrasts with the United States in the minicases above is the purpose or goal of dropout prevention and recovery. In the VET countries, the goal is not to get young people to complete upper secondary school, but to engage them in learning for jobs. This is quite a different matter—and one could argue much more attuned to the developmental needs of young people. Adolescents, especially those with a fragile sense of their own competence in the world, need experiences that test and confirm their abilities, and give them agency. School, by and large, does not meet this test. Jobs, even with apprenticeship wages, do, and jobs give such young people a pathway to the future, whereas school simply replicates the experiences that have often bored them in past years and resulted in failure and disengagement.

Absent a strong VET system in the United States, those programs that do attempt to connect struggling young people with training for work must fight all the battles on their own: they must develop a preparatory curriculum, simulate the workplace or seek work placements from sympathetic employers, and hope that without an apprenticeship wage students will be motivated to show up, and employers will be able to handle the likely eventualities. This is a far different proposition than developing programs for vulnerable students within a system where the majority are headed for a mix of schooling and work, and the social security system either provides incentives for participation or requires it. The pathways are already laid out for young people, the end point is an adult job, and the options are transparent for further education.

Conclusion

Possibilities in the United States

> Studying what other systems do is a worthwhile activity not because it gives us answers, but because it gives us questions and ideas. Careful comparative work raises new possibilities for any country to think about, and also allows us to see our own taken-for-granted practices with new eyes. It tells us that there are other ways to get to a goal and broadens our thinking about what these might be.
>
> —*Henry Levin*

The motivating idea for this book was to put before American educators and policy makers some examples of systems of education that get better results than the United States does for the large group of young people who do not opt for a university education. These are the young people who leave education in the United States—whether high school or community college—without a clear pathway into an occupation. The goal of the book is not just to provide a tourists' guide through what I have called "strong VET systems," but, as the quote above suggests, to "*allow [readers] to see our own taken-for-granted practices with new eyes.*" and to provoke them into considering that "*there are other ways to get to a goal.*" Today, young people in the United States are coming of age with the future uncertain in a country in economic crisis. Many rightly doubt that there will again be careers and professions that are stable and worth investing in, that they will have means to support a family. In this environment, all young people, not just those from low-income families or with weak academic preparation, need more structure, more information, more experience of work, and more support than ever before.

Strong VET systems succeed by heading the majority of young people into a combination of education and workplace learning. While the systems profiled generally include pathways into a university or technical higher education for graduates of VET programs, their orientation and aim is preparation for each young person for a vocation, the completion of a set of qualifications with currency in the labor market, not a degree for its own sake. By *qualification*, these systems mean not just a certificate or diploma signaling the completion of a program of study, but that the holder has the necessary competence to do a job in a specific occupational area. In general, to attain a qualification, the student has had to demonstrate that she or he has content knowledge and skill, as well as sufficient learning gained and demonstrated in a real-world work setting, to claim an identity as an IT technician, electrician, child-care worker, or graphic designer.

THE U.S. COLLEGE COMPLETION STRATEGY

As I have noted earlier in this book, the United States is pursuing a different strategy. After years of focus on improving high school graduation rates and college access (meaning matriculation into college), the goal now is attainment of a bachelor's degree, an associate's degree, or a certificate after completion of high school. One cannot really object—dropping out is wasteful and expensive. But the question is whether a completion agenda is the best way to get where we need to go. An alternative is to focus more attention and resources on the transition for young people from school, to learning to work, to careers—a model more like that in countries that have strong vocational education systems. This would likely result in more degree completion, but labor market viability would be the motivating factor.

Until the recent economic crisis, it has generally been the case that most middle-class young people without a postsecondary degree but with some college have been able to find their way into the primary labor market by their midtwenties. And those with a degree, whatever their major, rightly expected and got a return on their investment in a decent job and income. The result is that the cost of arriving at one's midtwenties without a postsecondary credential has been borne mostly by young people who have not had access to the kinds of family and social networks that can compensate for the lack of formal credentials. But as the labor market has tightened, businesses are seeking to fill vacancies with applicants whose credentials and experience are not just generally applicable—as are those of the good liberal arts graduate—but more precisely tailored to employer requirements. Hence the reports from states that their employers complain that college-educated job applicants do not have the applied skills to meet their needs.[1] Now it is not just young people at-risk, but middle- and upper-middle-class sons and daughters who are adrift in the labor market.

Consequently, by depending on a higher-education credential alone as the ticket to a job, we may be putting nearly half of our young people at risk in job market labeled "dismal" for college graduates in 2011. As I noted in the introduction, one-third of U.S. youth already fall into the categories established in the OECD's *Jobs for Youth* studies—*youth left behind* and *poorly integrated new entrants*, the latter phrase meaning the group will have difficulty settling into a permanent job. And the numbers are growing. States are cognizant of the dangers of having large numbers of young people floundering in the labor market—especially when skilled jobs with career ladders are going begging. For this reason alone, it is worth trying to understand how strong VET systems succeed in preparing and credentialing a much larger fraction of their young people for meaningful employment.

One could argue that the three characteristics of the strong VET systems that distinguish them from the United States' approach—a qualifications system, engaged employers, and workplace learning—are out of the realm of possibility in the U.S. economy, and that vocational education in high school has such a poor reputation for quality and as a dead-end destination for low-income young people that "college for all" is the only solution. In addition, many in the United States believe that asking young people to make a career decision at the age of sixteen, however strong the programs they enter, is presuming a maturity they don't yet have, and so forcing a choice that could have negative consequences. We could leave the argument there and accept tourist status and declare that systems abroad are exotic, impressive, and inaccessible. But that would be unfortunate.

STRONG U.S. CAREER PREPARATION INITIATIVES

In this concluding chapter, I briefly identify U.S. initiatives in high schools and postsecondary systems that are carefully preparing young people for careers—taking into account the career-specific knowledge needed; providing strong foundations in reading, writing, and math; and getting students at least some of the experiential learning and real-time problem solving that makes a difference in the labor market. The United States is not without excellent high school career and technical education (CTE) models, some replicated at considerable scale, and most with aspirations for both career and college readiness as the outcome. And many community colleges mount certificate and degree programs with clinical or internship requirements that do get completers excellent starting jobs. Indeed, evidence is growing that if you choose the right associate's degree, you can earn more than a good proportion of college graduates. Recent data from Florida, for example, shows that graduates with two-year associate in science degrees earned $10,357 more on average than BA graduates of the State University System.[2] Known and admired abroad for its inventiveness and entrepreneurial spirit in education as well as other areas, the United States has pockets of excellence. We just don't have a system.

High Schools

At the high school level, cutting-edge CTE bears little relationship to traditional vocational education programs that are sometimes little more than schools of last resort for students who were not going to succeed in college-prep. Indeed, today's best CTE programs do a better job of educating low-income and underprepared young people for college and career than traditional academics-only programs. National initiatives such as career academies, Big Picture Learning schools, Project Lead the Way, High Schools That Work, and Linked Learning—a more recent California initiative—combine the broad academic foundation needed for further education with some depth of study in a career area.

According to MDRC research, the career academy movement—the largest "modern" CTE program, now some seven thousand schools strong—helps graduates achieve higher earnings as adults. The academies introduce students to career themes and typically include workplace learning.[3] Project Lead the Way introduces high school students to engineering using a rigorous, uniform curriculum; national assessments; professional development for teachers; and extensive project-based learning, and can be installed within a traditional high school. It has now spread to over three thousand high schools. High Schools That Work (HSTW), developed by the Southern Regional Education Board (SREB), has grown into the nation's largest effort to integrate challenging academics and CTE. Currently, SREB is working to develop new, high-quality career-focused "programs of study," taking advantage of funding available through a provision in the U.S. Department of Education's Perkins legislation.

The newest of the modernized CTE models is Linked Learning, an ambitious California initiative that goes beyond career exploration in high school to provide engaging career concentration in areas in high demand in specific labor markets in the state—engineering, biomedical and health sciences, energy, information technology, manufacturing, natural resources, and the like. Linked Learning has developed an integrated and interdisciplinary curriculum and pathways into postsecondary education.[4]

With aspirations to engage employers and to place students in serious internship situations, Linked Learning has taken the unusual step to establish a special teacher preparation program since even teachers who enter the CTE from other careers may not have the skills to work in such programs, and traditionally trained teachers certainly don't. According to Linked Learning, teachers must be able to "design meaningful instructional tasks based on real-world problems, stay abreast of changes in their field, identify cross-sections between academic and career-technical focuses, coordinate school- and workplace learning, simulate workplace environments, identify career paths, and understand labor trends and projections."[5]

Two high-performing school networks for high school–age young people—Cristo Rey and Year Up—have commonalities with European apprenticeships: substantial work experience is a requirement for everyone, and students are socialized to understand and perform well in a business culture. Organized through its Corporate Work Study Program, Cristo Rey students work one day a week in hospitals, universities, law firms, research labs, and private businesses.[6] Serving high school graduates ages eighteen to twenty-four entering with weak skills, the yearlong Year Up program provides technical and professional skills, college credits, an educational stipend, and a six-month corporate internship.[7] Some high school CTE programs have certification and licensure requirements that include clinical or work-based experience evaluated as part of meeting completion requirements to meet state, national, or even international standards. City University of New York (CUNY) is starting a new community college designed on an entirely new work and learning model; students will prepare for a limited number of careers in high-need and high-value areas in New York City.

High School/College Hybrids

States are also linking high school and postsecondary education to support college-level credit in high school through dual-enrollment and accelerated whole school models such as early college high schools (ECHS). The recent rapid growth in dual-enrollment programs and the promising development of a national network of some 250 ECHS suggest that some of the barriers that have prevented better cooperation across the secondary/postsecondary boundary are beginning to break down. There are now over 53,000 young people in the ECHS network, the majority low-income students and students of color. Over 40 percent are graduating from high school with at least one year of college credit, and nearly a quarter with an associate's degree. About one-third of the programs have a science, technology, engineering, and mathematics (STEM) focus, with young people equipped to enter the job market after the associate's if they want to. North Carolina's Learn and Earn schools offer ECHS STEM and career-focused models with strong political support and employer participation that other states and districts could adapt to suit their education and employment needs.[8]

Postsecondary Institutions

Working up the education pipeline to community colleges, these too have many strengths and have the potential to be engines of career education for young people. The attention to these institutions over the last few years has highlighted both their assets and their challenges. The challenge is in the headlines: poor completion rates. Among the first issue to be confronted by educators seeking to improve outcomes is developmental education. Nearly 60 percent of all entrants are placed into noncredit remediation, many of them recent high school graduates. Indeed, fewer than 25 percent of developmental education students complete a certificate or degree within eight years of enrolling. Many never get beyond a remedial math course. Recent evidence from a California study shows that while community colleges mount career programs in high-wage fields—the researchers studied information technology, engineering technology, engineering, and nursing—those who complete the programs, and few do, are older and do not need developmental courses.[9] While more research is needed, the California study and other anecdotal evidence suggests that high schoolers with low to middling grades who finish remediation and make it into credit-bearing courses may not get through anatomy, math, basic IT courses, and similar prerequisites needed for high-value career certificates and degrees. Nonetheless, career education is strong in many community colleges, so there is much on which to build.

AN AMENDED FOCUS TO THE U.S. COMPLETION AGENDA

If there is any good news from the economic crisis, it is that such organizations as the National Governors Association (NGA) are arguing that the completion agenda should be driven by a state's economic development needs. Along with encouraging employers to join in shaping career education, the NGA asserts that while "any . . . degree is better than no degree . . . degrees that do not fit the . . . globalized and . . . knowledge-based job market . . . will not lift the economy."[10]

Several national philanthropies are turning their attention not just to completion, but to improved access to career preparation for young adults. Acting on a growing body of rigorous research, these initiatives are putting in place community college programs that get students started in a career pathway by embedding remediation in students' first occupation-related courses, providing fewer choices and more structure, and accelerating time to completion. This is a significant move in the right direction, and community colleges need the best resources and support to put in place these promising practices.[11]

In addition to such new approaches, numerous community colleges and four-year institutions have strong links to employers and provide service learning, internships, work study, co-op, and the like. One highly respected and successful model with more than "light touch" employer engagement is Northeastern University in Boston, Massachusetts. Northeastern began as an outgrowth of an education program run by the Young Men's Christian Association for the enormous immigrant community that entered Boston in the 1880s and '90s. From the start, Northeastern was practical; the first programs were evening courses in such areas as automobiles, law, finance, and a polytechnic school with cooperative engineering courses linked to workplaces. Fast-forward to the twenty-first century. Today Northeastern is a selective institution of nearly 14,000 students, nine in ten of whom complete at least one six-month co-op during their college years, and many up to three co-ops (eighteen months of work experience). Student choose from among the over 2,300 employers around the world who are committed to taking on Northeastern students. Nearly two-thirds of co-op students are offered jobs with their co-op employers upon graduation.

Employers of Northeastern students participate for the same reasons as employers do in the strong VET systems: they gain a pipeline to tested employees; the six-month time period allows students to learn enough to do productive work at a low cost, freeing up regular employees for new tasks. And employers benefit from the talent, enthusiasm, and ideas of young people. If the student is hired upon graduation, there are no recruitment costs. In today's economy, applications to Northeastern are booming—there were 43,000 applicants for 2,800 places in the 2011 first-year class. Co-op is the big draw.

THINKING ABOUT U.S. POSSIBILITIES

This is a book about strong VET systems outside of the United States, not a prescription for our country or a set of recommended actions. Nonetheless, I offer a few reflections that may be helpful to readers engaged enough with this topic to want some takeaways.

First, a promising strategy to engage U.S. employers in building a U.S. version of a strong VET system is to begin with community colleges and four-year colleges rather than with high schools. The primary labor market is not set up to absorb sixteen- to eighteen-year-olds in any substantial numbers, even as trainees; and most employers would be skeptical that young people at that age could make a productive contribution to the company's bottom line, whatever evidence you might show them from Switzerland or Germany or Australia. U.S. employers would be much more likely to embrace a program for young people that uses college enrollment as the initial screen, for this usually signals at least a certain level of perseverance and initiative.

Second, a jumping-off point for any serious conversation about building a system of career education in the United States is to acknowledge that a high proportion of college students are already both working and learning; the problem is that in all but a handful of cases, these two activities are competing with, rather than complementing, one another. U.S. students work while going to college in order to pay their bills. Except for institutions like Northeastern that offer "cooperative" programs in which the institution organizes job placements aligned with a student's academic program, paid student employment (as distinct from unpaid internships) is disconnected from the academic program, and students are forced to fit their work schedule around their academic course schedule rather than being able to plan these two sets of activities in an integrated fashion. Most students are not in "student-friendly" workplaces.

Third, any strategy aimed at engaging employers more deeply with postsecondary students should not ignore secondary-level CTE programs like the kinds of successful national models referenced earlier and such new models as early colleges, which link young people tightly to postsecondary education while they are still in high school. The ultimate goal should be to build career pathways that pick students up in the middle of high school and carry them through to at least a postsecondary occupational certificate or an associate's degree, if not a career-related BA. Programs that span grades 11–14 would not only align our CTE system with the age span covered in most strong VET systems, but enable a much more focused and efficient use of scarce federal and state funds that are too often divided among fragmented, uncoordinated, and competing programs at the secondary and postsecondary levels.

So where do the U.S. examples leave us? First, most young people go on to postsecondary education because they want to prepare for a career. Increasingly, they and their families know that work experience makes the difference in the labor market between getting a job and floundering to get a toehold. No one has to convince young people that completing high school and attaining a community college degree or a certificate with some work experience in a chosen career field is a must today and a good investment, even if you want to go on to a four-year institution or graduate school. The problem is that excellent but scattershot opportunities for young people do not constitute a system. And while each of the examples described earlier in this chapter has a U.S. version of some key element in strong VET systems, none has all of them. For either high school or community college programs, the following is a must-have list for improved designs:

- Employer and business leader engagement in design and support of effective pathways to careers
- Structured pathways with clear requirements, timelines, and outcomes leading from high school though postsecondary credential completion
- Opportunities to engage young people in workplace learning
- Effective career counseling and guidance, including scaffolded exposure to employers and career pathways beginning in the middle grades
- New institutional structures at the regional labor market level to provide coordination, quality assurance, and sustainability

How to conclude? Like so much that educators write, the news about our system of education is often either about extensive and profound failure or extraordinary success. And I fear I may be guilty of the latter crime in describing the best VET systems. Perhaps the best suggestion that I can make is that readers buy a plane ticket to one of the strong VET countries, talk to employers, see young people at work, and decide for yourself whether the system performs as described here. I suspect you will conclude that even put in terms of what are "good enough" rather than the best results, strong VET systems have an intriguing story to tell about what it takes for a country—employers, unions, educators, labor and social welfare systems—to make a policy commitment that all young people will be prepared for and launched into a calling or vocation.

Notes

Introduction

1. From S. Scarpetta, A. Sonnet, and T. Manfredi, "Rising Youth Unemployment During The Crisis: How to Prevent Negative Long-term Consequences on a Generation?" (OECD Social, Employment and Migration Working Papers, no. 106, OECD Publishing, Paris, 2010).

The difference between the United States and the EU19 average in the ratio of the minimum to median wage is even larger when the adult rate, mostly applicable to youth aged eighteen or older, is used. (The EU19 refers to all EU countries prior to the accession of the 10 candidate countries on 1 May 2004, plus the four eastern European member countries of the OECD, namely Czech Republic, Hungary, Poland, and Slovak Republic.) It is also noteworthy that, with few exceptions, unemployment benefits in the United States are contribution based (thus youth rarely qualify) and last for a maximum of six months, though in cyclical downturns this is usually extended to twelve months, as is the case during the current downturn in most states. On the other hand, eleven European countries grant access to unemployment benefits to youth without any work experience, although replacement rates tend to be small.

2. Ibid., 19.

3. Numerous research studies confirm the positive results of strong apprenticeship systems. See OECD, *Learning for Jobs* (Paris: OECD Publishing, 2010) and *Jobs for Youth* (Paris: OECD Publishing, 2010). Also see John H. Bishop, "Which Secondary Education Systems Work Best? The United States or Northern Europe" (working papers 2010, paper 105, Cornell University, Ithaca, N.Y. http://digitalcommons.ilr.cornell.edu/workingpapers/105); S. Lamb, "Alternative Pathways to High School Graduation: An International Comparison," California Dropout Research Project, report no. 7 (2008); and Kathrin Bertschy, M. Alejandra Cattaneo, and Stefan C. Wolter, "PISA and the Transition into the Labour Market," *Labour* 23, no. s1 (2009): 111–137.

4. OECD, *Jobs for Youth/Des Emplois Pour les Jeunes: The Netherlands, 2008* (Paris: OECD Publishing, 2008).

5. OECD, *Jobs for Youth*; OECD, *Tackling the Jobs Crisis* (Paris: OECD, 2009).

6. Anthony P. Carnevale, Jeff Strohl, and Nicole Smith, "Help Wanted: Postsecondary Education and Training Required," in *Occupational Outlook for Community College Students*, eds. Richard M. Romano and Hirschel Kasper, New Directions for Community Colleges, no. 146, (San Francisco: Jossey-Bass, 2009), 23.

7. OECD, *Learning for Jobs*, 105.

Chapter 1

1. Stefan Wolter and Paul Ryan, "Apprenticeship," in *Handbook of the Economics of Education*, eds. Eric A. Hanushek, Stephen Machin, and Ludger Woessmann (Amsterdam: Elsevier, 2010), 3:9.

2. "Key terms," European Qualifications Framework, Vocational Training, http://europa.eu/legislation_summaries/education_training_youth/vocational _training/c11104_en.htm; "National Qualifications Frameworks," Bologna Process, European Higher Education Area, http://www.ehea.info/article-details.aspx?ArticleId=69.

3. Anneke Westerhuis, *Bricklaying Country Report Netherlands*, Leonardo Da Vinci Project, Bricklayer (Netherlands: European Federation of Building and Woodworkers's-Hertogenbosch, 2008), 3.

4. Begun in a conference in Bologna, Italy, in 1999, the Bologna Process is an initiative to create a European Higher Education Area (EHEA) to facilitate mobility of students, graduates, and higher education staff and academic exchange. The work entails harmonizing degree content and requirements across the forty-seven countries currently signed on. See "About the Bologna Process," http://www.ond.vlaanderen.be/hogeronderwijs/bologna/.

5. W. Streeck, in Linda Clarke and Christopher Winch, "A European Skills Framework?—But What Are Skills? Anglo-Saxon Versus German Concepts," *Journal of Education and Work* 19, no. 3 (2006): 14, http://dx.doi.org/ 10.1080/13639080600776870.

6. Clarke and Winch, "A European Skills Framework?," 18.

7. BIBB (Bundesinstitut für Berufsbildung), AWEB "Berufliche Qualificationen—Spezialtiefbauer/bauerin," 1999, http://www.bibb.de.

8. Ibid., 16.

9. Westerhuis, *Bricklaying Country Report Netherlands*, 12.

10. Ibid., 13.

11. Ibid.

12. Ibid., 14.

13. *Procesmanagement Kwalificatiestructuur* (no date), *Nieuwe Kwalificatiestructuur: Opleiden tot vakmanschap en burgerzin* (Zoetermeer, Netherlands: COLO), translated and cited in Linda Clarke and Christopher Winch, "*Nuffield Study Crossnational Skills and Qualifications: Crossnational Synthesis*," Nuffield Foundation, http://www.nuffieldfoundation.org/cross-national-equivalence-vocational-skills-and-qualifications.

14. "Qualifications," About the AQF, Australian Qualifications Framework, http://www.aqf.edu.au.

15. Ibid.

16. Philippe Mehaut, "Key Concepts and Debates in the French VET System and Labor Market" (paper for the seminar "Developing a European Qualifications Framework—Conceptual and Labor Market Questions," Kings College, London, 2006), 3.

17. Ibid., 5.

18. "Vocational Education and Training (VET)," *Lifelong Learning Policy, European Commission Education and Training,* http://ec.europa.eu/education/lifelong-learning-policy/doc60_en.htm.

19. "The Copenhagen Declaration," Declaration of the European Ministers of Vocational Education and Training, and the European Commission, convened in Copenhagen, November 29 and 30, 2002, on enhanced European cooperation in vocational education and training.

20. The Relationship Between Quality Assurance and VET Certification in EU Member States, CEDEFOP Panorama Series (Luxembourg: Office for Official Publications of the European Communities, 2009), 7.

21. European Union, *Added Value of National Qualifications Frameworks in Implementing the EQF*, European Qualifications Framework Series, note 2 (Luxembourg: European Union, 2010), 16.

22. Loukas Zahilas, "The European Qualifications Framework (EQF): A Tool to Describe and Compare Qualifications," *Adapt Dossier*, no. 22 (November 2009): 5–8.

23. *CVET: From Principles to Practice, Synthesis Report*, European Commission, Directorate-General for Education and Culture, Paris, December 4–5, 2008, 14, http://ecvet.teamwork.fr/docs/.

24. Ina Dimireva, "Free Movement of People Within the EU," *EUbusiness*, last modified January 21, 2010, http://www.eubusiness.com/topics/living-in-eu/aggregator/free-movement/.

25. Ibid.

26. "What Is Liberal Education?" Association of American Colleges and Universities, http://www.aacu.org/leap/what_is_liberal_education.cfm.

Chapter 2

1. NCVER, *Australian Vocational Education and Training Statistics: Employers' Use and Views of the VET System 2009* (Adelaide, Australia: National Center for Vocational Education Research [NCVER], 2009).

2. Ibid.; Kathrin Hoeckel and Robert Schwartz, *Learning for Jobs: OECD Reviews of Vocational Education and Training, Germany* (Paris: OECD Publishing, 2010); and Kathrin Hoeckel, Simon Field, and W. Norton Grubb, *Learning for Jobs: OECD Reviews of Vocational Education and Training, Switzerland* (Paris: OECD Publishing, 2009).

3. Stefan Wolter and Paul Ryan, "Apprenticeship," in *Handbook of the Economics of Education*, vol. 3, eds. Eric A. Hanushek, Stephen Machin, and Ludger Woessmann (Amsterdam: Elsevier, 2010).

4. W. Streeck, J. Hilbert, K.-H. van Kevelaer, F. Maier, and H. Weber. *The Role of the Social Partners in Vocational Training and Further Training in the Federal Republic of Germany*, (Berlin: CEDEFOP, 1989); Norton Grubb, *Education Through Occupations*, (New York City: Teachers College Press, 1995); Paul Ryan, "The School-to-Work Transition: A Cross-National Perspective," *Jounral of Economic Literature,* 39, no. 1 (March 2001): 34–92. Simon Field, Victoria Kis, and Malgorzata Kuczera, *Learning for Jobs: OECD Reviews of Vocational Education and Training: Initial Report* (Paris: OECD Publishing, 2009); Stephen Nickell and Glenda Quintini, "The Consequences of the Decline in Public Sector Pay in Britain: A Little Bit of Evidence," *The Economic Journal* 112, no. 477, 2002.

5. Samuel Mühlemann et. al, "The Financing of Apprenticeship Training in the Light of Labor Market Regulations," *Labour Economics* 17, no. 5 (October 2010): 799–809.

6. Daimler AG, *Sustainability Newsletter,* November 2009, p. 3.

7. Małgorzata Kuczera et al., *Learning for Jobs: OECD Reviews of Vocational Education and Training, Sweden* (Paris: OECD Publishing, 2008), 10–19.

8. Simon Field, senior analyst in the Education and Training Policy Division, OECD's Directorate for Education, personal communication with author, 2010.

9. Table A1.2a, "Population That Has Attained at Least Upper Secondary Education (2006)," *Education at a Glance: OECD Indicators* (Paris: OECD Publishing, 2008), 43.

10. OECD, *Jobs for Youth/Des Emplois Pour les Jeunes: United Kingdom, 2008* (Paris: OECD Publishing, 2008), 28.

11. Alison Wolf, *Review of Vocational Education—The Wolf Report*, 2010, 51–52 and 63, https://www.education.gov.uk/publications/standard/publicationDetail/Page1/DFE-00031-2011.

12. Hanushek, Machin, and Woessmann, *Handbook of the Economics of Education*.

13. *Monopsony* is a state in which demand comes from one source. If there is only one customer for a certain good, that customer has a monopsony in the market for that good.

14. Mühlemann et al., "The Financing of Apprenticeship Training," 799–809.

15. OECD, *Jobs for Youth*, 125.

16. G. Quintini and T. Manfredi, "Going Separate Ways? School-to-Work Transitions in the United States and Europe" (OECD Social, Employment, and Migration working paper 90, OECD Publishing, Paris, 2009).

17. David N. F. Bell and David G. Blanchflower, *Youth Unemployment: Déjà Vu?* (Bonn, Germany: IZA, January 2010), 11.

18. Regina Dionisius et al., "Cost and Benefit of Apprenticeship Training: A Comparison of Germany and Switzerland," *Applied Economics Quarterly* 55, no. 1 (2009): 7–37.

19. Matthew Saltmarsh, "Global Youth Unemployment Reaches New High," *New York Times*, August 11, 2010.

20. OECD, *Learning for Jobs: OECD Reviews of Vocational Education and Training* (Paris: OECD Publishing, 2010), 121.

21. P. Lewis, *Minimum Wages and Employment*, report commissioned by the Australian Fair Pay Commission, Center for Labor Market Research, 2006.

22. Małgorzata Kuczera et al., *Learning for Jobs: OECD Reviews of Vocational Education and Training, Norway* (Paris: OECD Publishing, 2008).

23. "Minimum Wages for Youth, Students, and Trainees," *The Minimum Wage: Information, Opinion, Research*, http://www.raiseminwage.org/id37.html.

24. OECD, *Learning for Jobs*, 120.

25. Ibid., 122.

26. Conclusion adapted in part from William C. Symonds, Robert B. Schwartz, and Ronald Ferguson, *Pathways to Prosperity: Meeting the Challenge of Preparing Young Americans for the 21st Century*, Pathways to Prosperity Project (Cambridge, MA: Harvard Graduate School of Education, 2011).

27. These figures are taken from *Help Wanted: Projections of Jobs and Education Requirements Through 2018* (Washington, DC: Georgetown University Center on Education and the Workforce, 2010). See especially the introduction and part one.

Chapter 3

1. Towards a History of Vocational Education and Training (VET) in Europe in a Comparative Perspective: Proceedings of the First International Conference, October 2002, Florence, vol. 1, The Rise of National VET Systems in a Comparative Perspective, CEDEFOP Panorama Series (Luxembourg: Office for Official Publications of the European Communities, 2004), 20, 26.

2. Svenja Petersen, "Dual VET Systems in a Comparative Perspective— An Overview of Five OECD Countries," (unpublished paper, OECD, 2009).

3. Gisela Dybowski, "The Dual Vocational Education and Training System in Germany," Research and Service Concept Development/International Vocational Training/Education Marketing, Federal Institute for Vocational Education and Training (BIBB) (keynote speech at Dual Vocational Training International Conference, Taiwan, April 25, 2005), www.bibb.de/dokumente/pdf/a23_internationales_dybowski-taiwan_april-05.pdf.

4. *Facts and Figures: Vocational and Professional Education and Training in Switzerland 2010* (Bern, Switzerland: Federal Department of Economic Affairs, Federal Office for Professional Education and Technology), 15.

5. See OECD, *Learning for Jobs: OECD Reviews of Vocational Education and Training, Germany* (Paris: OECD Publishing, 2010) 43–53. The report makes numerous recommendations about how to address this challenge, which can set Germany behind in the global market place.

6. Ibid.

7. See the section "Germanic Countries" in chapter 1 of this book.

8. http://www.dihk.de/english/.

9. Margrit V. Zinggeler, "The Educational Duty of the German Chamber of Commerce," *Global Business Languages* 7, no. 1 (2002, reprinted 2010), http://Docs.Lib.Purdue.Edu/Gbl/Vol7/Iss1/9.

10. "Shaping Our Future: Australia's National Strategy for Vocational Education and Training 2004–2010," Australian National Training Authority, 3, http://www.dest.gov.au/sectors/training_skills/policy_issues_reviews/key_ issues/nts/dap/strategy.htm; OECD, Introduction to *Learning for Jobs: OECD Reviews of Vocational Education and Training, Australia* (Paris: OECD Publishing, 2008), 9.

11. NCVER, *Australian Vocational Education and Training Statistics: Employers' Use and Views of the VET System 2009* (Adelaide, Australia: National Center for Vocational Education Research [NCVER], 2009).

12. For more information on VET in Schools, see "What Is VET in Schools?" Department of Education, Employment, and Workplace Relations, Australian Government, http://www.deewr.gov.au/Schooling/CareersandTransitions/VocationalLearning/Pages/VocationalEducationin-Schools.aspx#whatisvet.

13. *Shaping Our Future, Australia's National Stratgy for VET 2004–10.* Australia National Training Authority, 2003.

14. "Australian Vocational Education and Training Statistics: Students and Courses 2010," NCVER, 2010, http://www.ncver.edu.au/publications/2383.html.

15. Peter Noonan, "The Future of VET: The Case for a New VET Settlement," in *The Future of VET: A Medley of Views*, eds. Francesca Beddie and Penelope Curtin (Adelaide, Australia: National Center for Vocational Education Research [NCVER], 2010), 18, http://www.ncver.edu.au/publications/2284.html.

16. "Systemic Innovation in the Australian VET System: Country Case Study Report," in *OECD/CERI Study of Systemic Innovation in Vocational Education and Training* (Paris: OECD Publishing, 2009), 5.

17. "The National Quality Council," http://www.nqc.tvetaustralia.com.au/about_nqc.

18. OECD, *Learning for Jobs: OECD Reviews of Vocational Education and Training, Norway* (Paris: OECD Publishing, 2008).

19. OECD, *Learning for Jobs*, 16. See also "Continuity and Change in Norwegian Vocational Education and Training (VET)," in *NIFU STEP Report 20/2008*, ed. Håkon Høst (Oslo: Norwegian Institute for Studies in Innovation, Research and Education [NIFU STEP], 2008), http://www.udir.no/upload/Rapporter/Fagopplaring/nifu_engelsk.pdf.

20. Data and analysis drawn from the following sources as well as a study visit to Rotterdam, April 2010: Johnny Sung, "Vocational Education and Training and Employer Engagement: An Industry-Led Sectoral System in the Netherlands," *International Journal of Training and Development* 14 (2010): 16–31; Dr. Peter van Ijsselmuiden, Ministry of Education, Culture and Science, "The System of Vocational and Adult Education in the Netherlands: How It Works, Major Development, Focus for the Future" (presentation for Hoffman in Rotterdam, April 2010); OECD, "Initial Education and On-the-Job Training," *Jobs for Youth/Des Emplois Pour les Jeunes: The Netherlands, 2008* (Paris: OECD Publishing, 2008), 57–95.

21. *Prepared for the Future: Dutch Qualifications for the Labor Market* (Netherlands: Colo, National Centers of Expertise on Vocational Education, Training and the Labor Market, 2008), http://www.colo.nl.

22. Sung, "Vocational Education and Training," 20.

23. Statistics Netherlands, http://www.cbs.nl/en-GB/menu/home/default.htm.

24. *Australian Qualifications Framework: Implementation Handbook*, 4th ed. (South Victoria: Australian Qualifications Framework [AQF] Advisory Board, 2007), 13.

25. "Information for Employers Overview," Australian Apprenticeships, Australian Government, http://www.australianapprenticeships.gov.au/Info_Emps/Overview.asp#1.

26. *Facts and Figures*, 19.

27. Stefan Wolter, professor of economics, University of Bern, Switzerland, personal e-mail communication with author, April 24, 2011.

28. "Opportunities for Internships and Apprenticeships in the Netherlands by Sector," *Colo Barometer of Practice Placements and Training on the Job* (Zoetermeer, Netherlands: Colo, [date]), http://www.colo.nl/publications.html.

Journal Essay: "The German Dual System"

1. For an in-depth review of Germany on which this journal draws, see Kathrin Hoeckel and Robert Schwartz, *Learning for Jobs: OECD Reviews of Vocational Education and Training, Germany* (Paris: OECD Publishing, 2010).

2. OECD, *Transition from Initial Education to Working Life* (Paris: OECD Publishing, 2004).

3. Stephen F. Hamilton, *Apprenticeship for Adulthood: Preparing Youth for the Future* (New York: Free Press, 1990).

Chapter 4

1. For example, see Mike Rose, *The Mind at Work: Valuing the Intelligence of the American Worker* (New York: Penguin, 2004); Matthew Crawford, *Shop Class as Soulcraft: An Inquiry into the Value of Work* (New York: Penguin, 2010); and the classic, Studs Terkel, *Working: People Talk About What They Do All Day and How They Feel About What They Do* (New York: New Press, 1997).

2. Yvonne Hillier, *Innovation in Teaching and Learning in Vocational Education and Training: International Perspectives* (Adelaide, Australia: National Center for Vocational Education Research [NCVER], 2009), 11.

3. Adapted from OECD, *Learning for Jobs: OECD Reviews of Vocational Education and Training* (Paris: OECD Publishing, 2010), 106.

4. Simon Field, senior analyst, Education and Training Policy Division, OECD, personal e-mail communication with author, June 10, 2010.

5. Samuel Mühlemann et al., "An Empirical Analysis of the Decision to Train Apprentices" (Economics of Education Working Paper Series 0005, University of Zurich, Institute for Strategy and Business Economics [ISU], 2005).

6. See *Report of SOMEC Coordinators on the Study Tour to Switzerland*, http://www.somec-moldova.org/0_somec/english/reports.eng/study_tour_CH_report.

7. Daniela Moser, "Developing Competences in Vocational Education: The Learn2act Research Project" (paper presented at the European Conference on Educational Research, Vienna, Austria, September 28–30, 2009).

8. Ibid., 6.

9. Martin Fischer and Waldemar Bauer, "Competing Approaches Towards Work Process Orientation in German Curriculum Development," *European Journal of Vocational Training*, no. 40 (2002): 142.

10. Jane Figgis, "Regenerating the Australian Landscape of Professional VET Practice: Practitioner-Driven Changes to Teaching and Learning," in *A National Vocational Education and Training Research and Evaluation Program Report* (Adelaide, Australia: NCVER, 2009), 16.

11. Kathrin Hoeckel, *Learning for Jobs: OECD Reviews of Vocational Education and Training, Austria* (Paris: OECD Publishing, 2010), 47.

12. Stefan Wolter, professor of economics, University of Bern, Switzerland, personal e-mail communication with author, May 15, 2011.

13. Figgis, "Regenerating the Australian Landscape."

14. Moser, "Developing Competences in Vocational Education."

15. Frank Levy and Richard J. Murnane, *The New Division of Labor: How Computers Are Creating the Next Job Market* (Princeton, NJ: Princeton University Press, 2004).

16. Figgis, "Regenerating the Australian Landscape," 10.

17. W. Norton Grubb, "The Richness of Occupational Instruction: The Paradox in the U.S. Community Colleges" (paper presented at Teaching and Learning Within Vocational and Occupational Education and Training Conference, Goettingen, Germany, 1999), 6–9.

18. W. Norton Grubb, "The Richness of Occupational Instruction: The Paradox in the U.S. Community Colleges" (paper presented at Teaching and Learning Within Vocational and Occupational Education and Training Conference, Goettingen, Germany, 1999), 37.

19. Ibid., 37.

20. Ibid., 39.

21. Both studies are cited in chap. 4, "Effective Teachers and Trainers," on which this paragraph draws; OECD, *Learning for Jobs, OECD Reviews of Vocational Education and Training* (Paris: OECD Publishing, 2010), 91–103.

22. Figgis, "Regenerating the Australian Landscape," 12.

23. In Germany, there are still separate academic and workplace final exams, and students receive separate grades for school exams and work exams. While the legal framework for VET requires teachers to contribute to the final chamber examination, which combines practical tasks and paper-and-pencil exams, the final chamber assessment tests only the occupation-specific competences of students. Broader academic knowledge imparted in the part-time schools is not directly part of the assessment. Thus, employers tend to look at the scores from the national exams set by the chamber or sectoral organization, not at the school exams.

24. Hoeckel, *Learning for Jobs*, 25.

25. "Effective Teachers and Trainers," *Learning for Jobs*, 91–103.

Journal Essay: "Ordinary Teenagers, Extraordinary Results"

1. Tonia Bieber and Kirsten Martens, "The OECD PISA Study as a Soft Power in Education? Lessons from Switzerland and the US," *European Journal of Education* 46, no. 1 (2011): part 1, 107, http://onlinelibrary.wiley.com/doi/10.1111/j.1465-3435.2010.01462.x/full.

2. Kathrin Bertschy, M. Alejandra Cattaneo, and Stefan C. Wolter, "PISA and the Transition into the Labour Market," *Labour* 23, no. s1 (2009): 111–137, http://ssrn.com/abstract=1378375.

Chapter 5

1. *Tackling the Jobs Crisis: The Labor Market and Social Policy Response, Theme 3, Helping Youth to Get a Firm Foothold in the Labor Market* (background document, Labor and Employment Ministerial Meeting, Paris, September 28–29, 2009).

2. David N. F. Bell and David Blanchflower (2009), *Youth Unemployment: Déjà Vu?*, www.dartmouth.edu/~blnchflr/papers/Youth%209-1.pdf. Bell and Blanchflower find evidence that spells of unemployment while people are young often create scars many years later through harmful effects on a number of outcomes: happiness, job satisfaction, wages, and health. Moreover, spells of unemployment tend to be particularly harmful to the individual—and to society—when the most disadvantaged youth become unemployed. This involves significant social as well as economic costs.

3. Niall O'Higgins, "The Impact of the Economic and Financial Crisis on Youth employment: Measures for Market Recovery in the European Union, Canada, and the United States," Employment Working Paper No. 70 (International Labour Office Employment Sector, Geneva, Switzerland, 2010), 1.

4. The comparison group is the European Union 19: Austria, Belgium, Czech Republic, Denmark, Finland, France, Germany, Greece, Hungary, Ireland, Italy, Luxembourg, Netherlands, Poland, Portugal, Slovak Republic, Spain, Sweden, United Kingdom. Note that neither Switzerland nor Norway is a member of the EU, and so they do not get included in these statistics; they have very strong results for youth employment.

5. Stefano Scarpetta, Anne Sonnet, and Thomas Manfredi, "Rising Youth Unemployment During the Crisis: How to Prevent Negative, Long-Term Consequences on a Generation?" (Social, Employment and Migration Papers, no. 106, OECD, Paris, April 2010), 13, figure 3. Also, *Jobs for Youth/Des Emplois Pour les Jeunes: United States* (Paris: OECD Publishing, 2009), 74. The youth unemployment rate in the United States has been below the OECD average since 1991. Until 2007, youth in the United States outperformed their OECD counterparts in the labor market: youth unemployment rarely lasted more than one year, and the share of NEET youth was slightly below the OECD average (see table 1.7). See the following url for updated information on the *Jobs for Youth* project: http://www.oecd.org/document/31/0,374 6,en_2649_37457_46328479_1_1_1_37457,00.html. Swiss youth unemployment rate, Swiss State Secretariat for Economics, monthly unemployment figures publication, German and French, http://www.seco.admin.ch.

6. Giorgio Brunello and Daniele Checchi' "Does school tracking affect equality of opportunity? New international evidence," *Economic Policy* 22, no. 52, 781–861, 2007. Brunelleo and Checchi found in a comparative study that countries that offered good-quality and attractive vocational training programs managed to reduce the impact of socioeconomic background on student attainment.

7. Most OECD countries do not keep racial or ethnic data, so they do not mark discrimination by U.S. categories. The prohibition against such data is a legacy from the Nazi period, when racial and ethnic data was used to identify and persecute members of minority groups.

8. European Parliament, 2009–2014, Committee on Employment and Social Affairs, draft report 2009/2221(INI) on promoting youth access to the labor market, strengthening trainee, internship, and apprenticeship status. The European Youth Guarantee is defined as "securing the right of every

young person to be offered a job, an apprenticeship, additional training or combined work and training after a maximum period of 6 months' unemployment" (p. 7). As of July 6, 2010, the parliament proposed that the period of unemployment be reduced to 4 months as a response to the economic crisis.

9. "Compact with Young Australians," Australian Government, April 2010, http://www.deewr.gov.au/Youth/YouthAttainmentandTransitions/Pages/compact.aspx.

10. "Compact with Young Australians: Questions and Answers," Australian Government, http://www.deewr.gov.au/Youth/YouthAttainmentandTransitions/Documents/CompactQAs.pdf.

11. This profile draws heavily on Kathrin Hoeckel, *Learning for Jobs: OECD Reviews of Vocational Education and Training, Austria* (Paris: OECD Publishing, 2010).

12. *Youth and Work in Austria* (Vienna: Federal Ministry of Labour, Social Affairs and Consumer Protection, 2010).

13. *The Approach to School Drop-out Policy in the Netherlands and the Results of the 2007–2008 Performance Agreements* (The Hague, Netherlands: Ministry of Education, Culture and Science, 2011), 5, http://www.aanvalopschooluitval.nl.

14. The Ministry of Education, Culture and Science leads the drive to reduce dropout rates. *Every Opportunity for Every Child: Youth and Family Programme* (The Hague, Netherlands: Ministry for Youth and Families, September 2007); *Annual Report 2009: National Youth Monitor* (The Hague, Netherlands: Statistics Netherlands, 2010). See http://www.aanvalopschooluitval.nl and http://www.voortijdigschoolverlaten.nl/english.php.

15. See http://www.aanvalopschooluitval.nl and http://youth.ituc-csi.org/Youth-Unemployment-and-How-to.

16. Act of 17 July 1998 no. 61 relating to Primary and Secondary Education and Training (the Education Act) with amendments in force as of 19 June 2009. In force as of 1 August 2009, Section 3-1: Right to upper secondary education and training for young people; Section 3-6: The follow-up service.

17. Torberg Falch et al., *Completion and Dropout in Upper Secondary Education in Norway: Causes and Consequences* (Trondheim: Center for Economic Research at NTNU, 2010).

18. C. Hall, "Does Making Upper Secondary School More Comprehensive Affect Dropout Rates, Educational Attainment and Earnings? Evidence from a Swedish Pilot Scheme" (IFAU working paper 2009:09, presented at the OECD, Reducing School Failure workshop, Uppsala, March 2010).

19. E. Markussen et al., "Completion, Drop-out and Attainment of Quali-fication in Upper Secondary Vocational Education in Norway," in *Continuity and Change in Norwegian Vocational Education and Training (VET)*, ed. H. Høst (Oslo: Norwegian Institute for Studies in Innovation, Research and Education [NIFU STEP], 2010), 31–53.

20. Ludwig Gärtner, *Child and Youth Policy in Switzerland*, http://www.coe.int/t/dg4/youth/Source/Resources/Forum21/Issue_No12/N12_Child_and_YP_Switzerland_en.pdf.

21. U. Haeberlin, C. Imdorf and W. Kronig, "Chancenungleichheit bei der Lehrstellensuche. Der Einfluss von Schule, Herkunft und Geschlecht," Schweizerische Koordinationsstelle für Bildungsforschung, Bern/Aarau, cited in OECD, *Learning for Jobs: OECD Reviews of Vocational Education and Training, Switzerland* (Paris: OECD Publishing, 2010), 30.

22. Drawn from OECD, *Learning for Jobs: OECD Reviews of Vocational Education and Training, Switzerland* (Paris: OECD Publishing, 2010).

23. "Systemic Innovation in the Swiss VET System: Country Case Study Report," *Study of Systemic Innovation in VET* (Paris: OECD/CERI, 2008), 13–17; "Developments," The Swiss Education Server, educa.ch, http://www.educa.ch/en/developments-2.

Conclusion

1. Erin Sparks and Mary Jo Waits, *Degrees for What Jobs? Raising Expectations for Universities and Colleges in a Global Economy* (Washington, DC: NGA Center for Best Practices, 2011), 8.

2. As the Miami Dade College (MDC) *College Forum* notes, "These data attest to the value of these programs in preparing students for high-demand, high-paying careers in a wide variety of industries. A few of these many fields and jobs include: Business—accounting technology and business administra-tion; Creative—computer design technology and radio and television broad-casting; Health care—nursing, physician assistants and specialized medical technicians; and, High-tech—networking service technician, Microsoft da-tabase administration and computer-aided drafting and design." See "MDC De-grees, Certificates Pay Off for Graduates," *College Forum* 15, no. 2 (April 2011).

3. J. Kemple, 2008. Career Academies: Long-Term Impacts on Labor Market Outcomes, Educational Attainment, and Transitions to Adulthood. New York, NY: MDRC.

J. Kemple, and J. Snipes, *Career Academies: Impacts on Students' Engagement and Performance in High School* (New York: MDRC, 2010).

4. Gary Hoachlander and Dave Yanofsky, "Making STEM Real," *Educational Leadership* 68, no. 6 (March 2011).

5. "Teacher Preparation for Linked Learning," ConnectEd, The California Center for College and Career, http://www.connectedcalifornia.org/services/teacherprep.php.

6. See Cristo Rey Network, http://www.cristoreynetwork.org/.

7. See Year Up, http://www.yearup.org/.

8. For the most recent data on early colleges, see Michael Webb and Lia Mayka, "Unconventional Wisdom: A Profile of the Graduates of Early College High School," *Jobs for the Future*, March 2011, http://www.jff.org/publications/education/unconventional-wisdom-profile-graduates-/1205. See also descriptions of a number of early college and community college initiatives at *Jobs for the Future*, http://www.jff.org.

9. Nancy Shulock, Colleen Moore, and Jeremy Offenstein, *The Road Less Travelled: Realizing the Potential of Career Technical Education in the California Community Colleges* (Sacramento, CA: Institute for Higher Education Leadership and Policy, California State University, Sacramento, 2011).

10. See Sparks and Waits, *Degrees for What Jobs?*, 11.

11. "Completion by Design Concept Paper," Postsecondary Success, Bill & Melinda Gates Foundation, September 2010, http://www.completionbydesign.org/; Lumina Foundation's publications under "Workforce Development," http://www.luminafoundation.org/newsroom/topics.html?_stopic=10.

About the Author

Nancy Hoffman is a vice president and senior advisor at Jobs for the Future, a national nonprofit in Boston, the mission of which is to improve educational and workforce outcomes for low-income young people and adults. She works on the Early College High School Initiative and state policy supporting high school and postsecondary completion. Hoffman serves as a consultant for the Education and Training Policy unit of the Organization for Economic Cooperation and Development (OECD). She has held teaching and administrative posts at Brown, Temple, Harvard, FIPSE, MIT, and elsewhere. She holds a BA and PhD from the University of California, Berkeley in comparative literature. Recent books include *Women's True Profession: Voices from the History of Teaching* (2003), *Double the Numbers: Increasing Postsecondary Credentials for Underrepresented Youth* (with Kazis and Vargas, 2004), and *Minding the Gap: Why Integrating High School with College Makes Sense and How to Do It* (with Vargas, Venezia, and Miller, 2007). Hoffman serves on the Massachusetts Board of Higher Education.

About the Contributor

Robert B. Schwartz is the Frances Keppel Professor of Practice at the Harvard Graduate School of Education and codirector of the Pathways to Prosperity project. He held a wide variety of leadership positions in education and government before joining the HGSE faculty in 1996. From 1997 to 2002, Schwartz also served as president of Achieve, Inc. Schwartz serves as a consultant to the OECD, and cochairs the Aspen Institute Program on Education and Society. Schwartz has written and spoken widely on standards-based reform, public-private partnerships, and the transition from high school to adulthood.

Index